Affirmative Gay Relationships
Key Steps in Finding a Life Partner

HARRINGTON PARK PRESS
Southern Tier Editions
Gay Relationships
Neil Kaminsky, LCSW, Senior Editor

Affirmative Gay Relationships: Key Steps in Finding a Life Partner
by Neil Kaminsky

ADDITIONAL HARRINGTON PARK PRESS TITLES
OF RELATED INTEREST

When It's Time to Leave Your Lover: A Guide for Gay Men
by Neil Kaminsky

Longtime Companions: Autobiographies of Gay Male Fidelity
edited by Alfred Lees and Ronald Nelson

Navigating Differences: Friendships Between Gay and Straight Men
by Jammie Price

Gay and Gray: The Older Homosexual Man, Second Edition
by Raymond M. Berger

Reeling in the Years: Gay Men's Perspectives on Age and Aging
by Tim Bergling

Growth and Intimacy for Gay Men: A Workbook by Christopher
J. Alexander

*Behold the Man: The Hype and Selling of Male Beauty in Media
and Culture* by Edisol Wayne Dotson

The Mentor: A Memoir of Friendship and Gay Identity by Jay Quinn

*The Gay Male's Odyssey in the Corporate World: From
Disempowerment to Empowerment* by Gerald V. Miller

*Fatherhood for Gay Men: An Emotional and Practical Guide
to Becoming a Gay Dad* by Kevin McGarry

Neil Kaminsky, LCSW

Affirmative Gay Relationships
Key Steps in Finding a Life Partner

Pre-publication
REVIEWS,
COMMENTARIES,
EVALUATIONS . . .

"If you are a gay man who feels hopeless about your intimacy prospects, stop complaining, stop blaming, and start reading. Neil Kaminsky offers sage relationship advice in a voice that is equal parts friendly, funny, and firm."

Greg Merrill, MSW
*Instructor, Gay Male
Relationships Course,
Department of Gay and Lesbian Studies,
City College, San Francisco*

"If finding long-lasting relationships were easy or simple, for any lifestyle, then all we would need is one book on the subject. But, as we know, there are shelves of books about relationships because they are complex and often elusive. Add to that the pressures placed on gay relationships and a healthy long-lasting gay relationship may seem impossible. *Affirmative Gay Relationships: Key Steps in Finding a Life Partner*, by Neil Kaminsky, gives the hope that with careful consideration we can make the choices that will lead us to a partner with whom we can share our lives. Yes, finding a partner is complex and requires an awareness of who we are, but this book guides us step-by-step through the process.

While many go through the cycle of getting together and breaking up only to end up blaming the other guy for what went wrong, this book brings it back to the reader and what choices the reader must make to take control of finding a life partner. Kaminsky has us focus on what we can do, how we can take responsibility, and in some cases how we need to get out of our own way when looking for a long-lasting relationship. He shows us that finding a life partner is serious work, but not unattainable.

Affirmative Gay Relationships: Key Steps in Finding a Life Partner is just what those who read Kaminsky's last book, *When It's Time to Leave Your Lover*, would expect—a useful, practical guide that does not feel like a classroom lecture. Kaminsky uses his years of experience and success working with gay men to empower his readers to find their own life partner."

Rick C. Roberts, MA
*Department of Communication Studies,
University of San Francisco*

Affirmative Gay Relationships
Key Steps in Finding a Life Partner

Neil Kaminsky, LCSW

Southern Tier Editions
Harrington Park Press®
An Imprint of The Haworth Press, Inc.
New York • London • Oxford

Published by

Southern Tier Editions, Harrington Park Press®, an imprint of The Haworth Press, Inc., 10 Alice Street, Binghamton, NY 13904-1580.

Cover design by Lora Wiggins.

Library of Congress Cataloging-in-Publication Data

Kaminsky, Neil, 1951-
    Affirmative gay relationships : key steps in finding a life partner / Neil Kaminsky.
        p. cm.
    Includes bibliographical references and index.
        ISBN 1-56023-362-1 (hard : alk. paper)— ISBN 1-56023-363-X (soft : alk. paper)
    1. Gay male couples—United States. 2. Dating (Social customs)—United States. 3. Interpersonal relations—United States. 4. Mate selection—United States. I. Title.
HQ76.2.U5 .K36 2003
646.7'7'086642—dc21

                                                                        2002027284

In memory of my beloved parents,
Gussie and Louis Kaminsky

ABOUT THE AUTHOR

Neil Kaminsky, LCSW, is a psychotherapist, writer, and lecturer who specializes in gay male issues. He is the author of *When It's Time to Leave Your Lover: A Guide for Gay Men.* He lectures throughout the country and has facilitated workshops for gay men at The L.A. Gay and Lesbian Center and New Leaf—Services For Our Community in San Francisco. He is a frequent guest speaker at City College of San Francisco, and has been a guest on radio and television.

Mr. Kaminsky received his BA in psychology from The State University of New York at Stony Brook and his MSW from New York University. He has a social work license both in New York and California.

Mr. Kaminsky lives in West Hollywood, California, where he is in private practice and a freelance writer. He is working on another book among other writing projects.

CONTENTS

Acknowledgments

As a therapist, writer, and public speaker, I endeavor to positively influence others. One of the great joys of this work is the good tidings that return. The gay men who are my clients, who are in my audiences, and who are my interviewees expand my perspective. As such, they enhance my life. I am grateful for the privilege of meeting so many fine individuals.

Thanks to my colleagues, those whose quotes appear in this book, and the many others who unselfishly gave their time, knowledge, and warm support. I'm deeply honored to be in a club with such members.

Thanks to my partner Virgilio—if I didn't thank him, I'd never hear the end of it!

Only kidding. He's a wonderful soul, and I'm truly blessed.

The person to whom I owe the most gratitude, however, is my mom. Gussie Kaminsky passed away on March 18, 2001. She was my best friend and simply the best mom on Planet Earth. She was a person who was *instinctively good and caring and loving*. Born in 1913, she wasn't privy to many affirmative visions of gay life. But when I came out to her at age twenty-five, she wholeheartedly embraced me and my lifestyle. When I told her of my fear that I would somehow be "disowned," she asked in her typical Brooklyn Jewish accent, "What . . . are you crazy?" During a ten-year relationship I began a few years later, she never held a conversation with me in which she didn't ask about my partner and remind me to tell him she said hello. When HIV appeared, she donated money. I recently found a note to me she attached to a donation (she had me send in the check) that said "with G-d's help, they'll find a cure."

Oh, she had expressed some unkind words in her life, but they were reserved for the likes of people such as Jerry Falwell. Anyone who would hurt her son and "his friends" was no friend of my mom!

She was a class act and a woman of enormous grace. You couldn't help but like her because she didn't just make you feel that she cared about you—*she really did care.* In the little town in Florida where she retired—from the people in the bank to those in her doctor's office to the ladies in the library—she was truly loved and is sorely missed.

The compassion and love in my life come from her.

Thank you, Mom. Thank you for being the best mom in the whole wide world.

Happy travels.

Your son, Neil.

Introduction

Gay men are looking for life partners. Visit any city, town, or Web site and the message is clear: we want to connect. We want to be in love. We want to live in a committed union with another gay man.

With such a strong, collective yearning, and in a society that has witnessed unprecedented gay affirmative change, you'd think this would be an easy endeavor.

It's not. Scores of us remain single. Many have suffered through multiple relationships that ended in heartache. Too many of us are resigned to the belief that real love is just an elusive dream.

This book is about shattering that supposition. It's about helping you find a real life partner. That, of course, is predicated on believing that he exists. This book will illustrate that he does, and what you can do to find him.

A **Real** *Life Partner*

Real is the operative word—a partner who wants to be there, someone in it for the long haul, a guy who understands what a relationship means, a man of essence not just sparkle, someone who can meet your emotional, intellectual, and spiritual needs, as well as your physical ones.

Much of what is thought of as "love" involves confused ideas fueled by fantasy, sexual fascination, and unrealistic expectations. Many guys who say they want a boyfriend are not ready, willing, or able to have one. Plenty don't have a clue about what's really involved. Many fear intimacy, are plagued by internalized homophobia, and create self-fulfilling prophecies of relationship doom.

This need not be. You and the men you encounter can gain clarity, understand and prepare for what's ahead, overcome homophobia, and develop hopeful expectations. This book explores how to accomplish these goals.

1

The Focus Is on You, Not "Them"

This book is about taking individual responsibility and harnessing your power to find love. Many of us don't want to face ourselves in the mirror. We credit "other gay men," "them," as the cause of our woes. "There are too many losers, too few quality gay men left," goes the cry. We don't see or don't want to see that we're talking about ourselves because *there is no "them." "Them" is you and me.*

This book takes the view that finding a life partner is mostly about growing from within. It's about *making different, affirmative choices,* which are key to creating new and better outcomes. If what you've been doing is not helping you find love, you have to do something different. Continuing to complain and believe in the sparse availability of gay men will get you absolutely nowhere.

Of course, there are inappropriate men to keep away from, and we'll explore how to identify them. But you have to take responsibility for preventing their access. It's you who has to turn down guys who offer short-term sexual charm and long-term relationship poison.

The book will also help you figure out what signs demonstrate availability and suitability for a committed relationship. But again, you must figure out what you want and need from a partner, and then invest the energy it takes to find him. You need to deal with your issues of trust, intimacy, and vulnerability.

This book devotes considerable space to helping you achieve these goals.

Ultimately, *Affirmative Gay Relationships* is about empowering you. It's about identifying and marshalling the most important means by which you will find a real life partner: the resources within *yourself.*

Chapter 1 speaks to the dissatisfaction those seeking partners experience, and introduces the main theme of the book: what the *individual* does or doesn't do essentially determines whether he finds love. It also presents some of the principal impediments to finding a life partner (difficulty with trust, preoccupation with youth and beauty, fear of rejection, etc.) which are explored in more detail in subsequent chapters.

Chapter 2 describes some of the characteristics needed for a committed relationship. Willingness to let go of the single life, emotional maturity, and the ability to tolerate the anxiety of intimacy are among the topics explored. The reader is then coached to identify his personal requirements for a partner. Examples of realistic and unrealistic requirements are described.

Chapter 3 describes gay men's obsession with youth and physical beauty and how this can interfere with meeting viable partners. The reader learns ways to accept himself and others.

Chapter 4 describes how feeling and appearing "desperate" can prevent meeting others. It explores some of the beliefs that fuel this anxiety, and instructs the reader in a number of ways to reduce unease in social gatherings.

Chapter 5 highlights some of the characteristics of availability or unavailability for a serious commitment. The reader will be able to look at both himself and prospective partners. Some examples of unavailability include men who are chronically angry, men who are too busy with other life pursuits, and men who have not grieved the end of a previous relationship. The questions of long distance relationships as well as relocating for a relationship are also explored.

Chapter 6 describes some of the positive, life-affirming aspects of being in love, but it also addresses what takes place in the "day-to-day" life of a relationship. Bilateral decision making, managing separateness and merging, and being "exposed" are explored. The chapter addresses how to realistically prepare for what's involved in a relationship.

Chapter 7 helps the reader conceptualize the kind of a relationship he's looking for exploring his core values. An exercise in which the reader imagines himself on his death bed is used to illustrate what is personally important. The reader is also asked to think in very specific terms about the kind of life he's seeking with a partner.

Chapter 8 explores the concept of a self-fulfilling prophecy and how negative expectations can result in *creating* what is expected. The reader learns to appreciate the role of his behavior in a self-fulfilling prophecy, and understands that he can choose to change his behavior. The reasons for negative expectations are examined as are strategies to change defeatist beliefs.

Chapter 9 discusses ways to prepare for meeting people. It emphasizes the importance of being comfortable when socializing. It examines a wide array of environments where men can meet, exploring advantages and disadvantages. The chapter explains why some places are less conducive to meeting while emphasizing the individual's power in making connections.

Chapter 10 explores the common fear of rejection and argues why it's essentially irrational. The reader is offered strategies to conquer fear and free himself to approach whomever he desires.

Although aiming high is the goal, Chapter 11 discusses how having unrealistic requirements can be counterproductive. It also describes some of the less than perfect aspects of relationships, such as seeing someone's "ugly side," making mistakes, and experiencing rocky times with no guarantees of resolution.

Chapter 12 examines the lack of control, need to trust, and risk of being hurt intrinsic to intimacy. Many gay men (and heterosexual men) have considerable difficulty accepting this emotional vulnerability. It argues that this is requisite for a viable relationship, and the reader will be helped to embrace it. The issue of trust is explored, including how to assess the trustworthiness of another.

Chapter 13, the last, discusses dating. Dating anxiety and anxiety management are addressed, and the importance of using this time as an assessment period is emphasized. The chapter focuses on what the reader has learned about himself from previous chapters. A significant number of questions are posed to help the reader figure out if he's courting someone who has what it takes to become his real life partner.

The Term "Life Partner"

The book focuses on creating and executing a well-thought-out plan to find a partner and form a healthy relationship. The hope is that it will be long term and maybe even for life. But sometimes the best of plans go wrong and a relationship that once worked no longer does. Staying together in such a situation is more like having a "life sentence." I think of a life partner as *someone who materially enhances your life,* not necessarily someone who will be with you for life.

Use of Quotes and Vignettes

Quotes from different gay men cited in the book came from responses to questionnaires I developed. The identifying information has been altered to protect privacy. The mental health professionals quoted are identified by their real names and other identifying information about them is real. All vignettes are fictional—the people and situations are composites based on my experiences.

Disclaimer

This book is written to help gay men find real life partners. However, there is no guarantee that reading this book will achieve that goal.

I am a licensed clinical social worker in California and have had many years of experience working with gay men as a therapist in private practice. With my knowledge of human behavior and professional experience, within the scope of my field I will at times explore certain emotional issues (such as anxiety and low self-esteem). There will also be a number of occasions when I will suggest the reader consider seeking professional help or join a self-help group. However, no claim is being made or implied that I am able to give comprehensive, specific advice about particular situations. No claim is being made or implied that this book can be a substitute for psychotherapy or any other kind of professional intervention, nor that the book can be used to self-diagnose anything. This book may work as a good adjunct along with psychotherapy. If you are in therapy, discuss this with your therapist. In addition, please note that I have no medical training; no form of medical advice is being given or implied.

Chapter 1

So Many Men, So Much Aggravation

The most common question I'm asked is, "How can I find a lover?" ... But if you look at how people are actually living their lives, they're avoiding it in every way possible.

Thomas Moon, MFT
Private Practice, San Francisco, California

It's an exciting time to be a gay man in the United States. Love, if not in the air, is certainly more obtainable than ever before.

We have begun the twenty-first century more powerful and more visible than any time in history. In such an era, opportunities to meet and fall in love are vast.

The Internet has opened a plethora of prospects. Any gay man who has a computer can meet other gay men. Organizations of almost every conceivable interest have sprung up across the land. As attitudes have changed, further opportunities have been created. Meeting a life partner in the grocery store, at work, or at your local café is not uncommon.

Gay bars and gay clubs across the United States continue to provide venues to find partners. Although these places present challenges because of the emphasis on quick sex, more than a few gay men have their found lovers in such surroundings.

Many gay men place love at the pinnacle of their life's goals. They know that a relationship can offer fulfillment unparalleled by most other human experiences.

So why aren't all of us in relationships? Why aren't all of us surrounded by conjugal bliss? Why is the picket fence, Prince Charming, and a ride off into the glorious sunset still only a dream for many?

The answers to these questions can be found in what we as gay men do or don't do to establish partnerships. Despite our pleas for love, many of us have deeply ambivalent feelings about getting involved. We are ambivalent about the objects of our love, namely gay men. The good news is that we can fall in love and have wonderful relationships. The salient point is that *we can create wonderful relationships in our lives.* The challenging issue is that we have to revamp many beliefs and take responsibility for making it happen. *The answer can no longer be that there is no one out there.* We have to look within.

A good starting point is exploring how we feel about other men. Countless numbers of us are not pleased with our fellow gay men. Many of you reading this book would say that is a gross understatement.

Running from Intimacy

Grievances are pervasive. Intimacy, a pivotal component of any serious relationship, probably tops the list of challenges.

Consider the following scenario: You find yourself falling in love with your boyfriend. Perhaps you have been dating for a few months. As you desire to see your relationship grow, you also sense that something is wrong. Your boyfriend tells you that he also wants to get close, but demonstrates behavior that is distancing. Indeed, the harder you try, the more he seems to pull away. When you question him about this, he says that he's really afraid to get close, that he's been hurt before, and that he needs more time before he can trust you. You accept that and are willing to give him time. However, more weeks and months don't cure the problem. When you broach the issue again, he announces that he really doesn't know what he wants, that maybe he needs some time away from you to sort things out. Perhaps, he says, he's not really ready for a relationship after all. He's sorry if this caused you any grief!

The Phone Call You Never Get

Another point of contention is the infamous promise to call that never materializes. You meet an attractive man. You have a wonderful conversation, everything seems to click, and you are terribly interested in seeing him again. He tells you he wants to see you as well. However, he can't give you his phone number because he's staying with a friend, doesn't have a phone yet, is never home (fill in the blank). His reasoning seems sensible and so you give him your phone number.

And never hear from him again.

The Breakup Fight

An argument that leads to an abrupt ending of a relationship is another way many of us become embittered with our brethren. It often goes something like this: In the midst of an altercation he announces he's leaving because he "can't take it anymore." Without any warning, it seems, your life has been turned upside down. The plans, the dreams, the future with him are obliterated in a flash. When this happens, you may wonder if he ever really loved you. You may resolve (consciously or unconsciously) never to permit another man to hurt you again.

Trust and Honesty

Lack of trust and honesty is another extremely disheartening experience for many gay men. How many of us have met guys who swore on their grandmothers' graves that they were being faithful, only to find out that they, apparently, were not terribly fond of their departed grandmothers? Many gay men actually expect their lovers to "cheat," which in effect means they expect them to be dishonest.

The Unwelcome Surprise

Shock and disappointment are further minefields we encounter in our quest for partnerships.

At first your new man seems like *the one,* and you are intoxicated with hope and wonderment, but then the roof comes crashing in when you discover that:

- he just wants to be friends
- he wants to date others
- he never thought he was dating you in the first place
- he's moving to another state
- he isn't over his ex
- his ex isn't really his ex

- he needs a little too much "space," like a continent
- he has some other problem that sinks your budding relationship

All of this is tiring, demoralizing, and enraging, and it may appear obvious from the examples I gave that the cause of the problem is once again *them*. The examples do indeed describe bad things done by others to you and me, but those others *are* ultimately you and me. It gets done to us, but we also do it to others. There is no secret society of "them." Often we justify our less than honorable behavior because we have been the recipients of the same. This is the royal road to nowhere. Stopping this merry-go-round is where to begin if you are seriously interested in finding a real life partner.

This doesn't mean that there aren't many unsuitable gay men. They are certainly out there. But there are also many good men; guys who are looking for the nonflake just as you are. Acknowledging that the power to find love resides within yourself will be the way you avoid the bad guys and meet the right ones.

Following is an outline of some of the crucial problems that create obstacles in meeting viable partners. Subsequent chapters will address some of these issues in detail along with strategies to overcome these challenges.

It's All About You Again!

The most important roadblock to finding a partner is the "personal responsibility issue" I have been hammering away at. You can't go on believing that the lack of suitable partners is what's keeping you from meeting Mr. Right. You have to truly believe that the power to meet or not meet resides primarily within yourself. This may not be easy if you are accustomed to seeing the cause for your distress or good fortune outside of yourself. This principle of personal responsibility is addressed throughout the book along with a good deal of evidence to support it. One way to reach this conclusion is to be open to considering my arguments—something which initially may seem difficult to do.

Self-Fulfilling Prophecy

Another problem is the multitude of negative expectations gay men have about gay relationships. Internalized homophobia does play a part, but many of us can recall very painful—sometimes traumatic—experiences we have had with lovers. Nothing is more lethal than negative expectations that become self-fulfilling prophecies. A self-fulfilling prophecy is something you so strongly believe *that you go about creating, without realizing,* that in which you believe. With inappropriate partners, you tend to feel attracted to those who are unavailable or in myriad other ways are not suitable (people who are dishonest, in a relationship and having clandestine affairs, addicted to drugs, emotionally immature, etc.). The suitable people never cross your attention threshold. These men may be literally in front of your face, but you don't see them. They may seem uninteresting or physically unattractive to you (yes, this process can actually make you feel physically unattracted to someone), or you may do something (imply you are unavailable, etc.) or not do something (not think of asking for his phone number, etc.), to simply prevent a connection from taking place. It's amazing how we can sabotage our happiness without realizing it! Most maddening about this is that the result—meeting another guy who turns out to be a jerk or meeting no one—becomes the "evidence" as to why you will "never find anyone." However, it is really evidence that you are creating a self-fulfilling prophecy! Self-fulfilling prophecies are rarely conscious, so it's all the more difficult to see the real dynamics that are operating. We will focus on this process later in the book.

Emotional Vulnerability/Loss of Control

Another issue is emotional vulnerability. When you love, you can be hurt badly. Real love means intimacy. It means bonding on an exceedingly deep level with another human being. This is certainly what we strive for when we look for a partner, but it doesn't come without a price. If he knows you very well, he also knows your weaknesses and the parts of you that are not very pretty. He's privy to those aspects that can be scary and embarrassing even for you to know. Being in love also implies dependency to some degree and curtailment of freedom. If you are in love with him you also need him and are accountable to him. To give someone such access puts you, to a certain degree, out of control. Your lover can attack your weaknesses, reveal them to the world, and think poorly of you, which matters because you love him. He can also leave you or die. All of these situations will create profound loss and pain. Men in our culture are powerfully socialized into "being in control" all of the time. Although many of us consciously reject this view, it lives on because of the pervasive sexist messages we were and are exposed to. Indeed, one could make the argument that because our masculinity has always been questioned, loss of control is even more difficult for gay men to accept. Thus, to embrace emotional vulnerability can be very difficult for us.

One example of how this manifests is the "getting scared of getting close phenomenon." It goes something like this: All seems to have been going well between two gay men and then rather abruptly one or both men find a way to destroy the relationship. It may come from a lie, a feeling of losing one's freedom, a decision that one wants to see others, or innumerable other problems that somehow sink the relationship. It's not that such men consciously decide to sabotage their budding union. However, if you peer below the surface, if you look at the operative psychodynamics, that's exactly what's happening. The loss of the relationship, as bad as that may seem, *brings about tremendous anxiety reduction*. Some gay men have so much difficulty with this that they never let a relationship begin. These are the people who almost never go out with anyone and will engage predominantly in anonymous encounters. Many of these men often believe it's the lack of available partners that's keeping them single. They are partially correct. *They* are unavailable.

Trust Again

A collateral issue is trust. To experience deep emotional closeness means you have to profoundly trust another. If you don't have this feeling, the kind of intimacy so special and unique in a love relationship won't be there. You literally cannot have one without the other.

When we have negative expectations of our relationships, negative feelings about our fellow gay men, and bad experiences in our past, it will be difficult to trust on such a level. Thus, a relationship may never get off the ground, or one or both of the men may bail when faced with this challenge. Again, this is likely to operate unconsciously and to manifest just when things seem to be developing. One or both men may begin to feel "uncomfortable" and do something that results in the demise of the relationship.

Of course, plenty of people really *shouldn't* be trusted. The trick is to separate real untrustworthiness from a belief that anyone and everyone is suspect. How to assess the integrity of another, and the relationship between your own trustworthiness and that of a potential mate are explored later in the book.

Trust, furthermore, never comes with any guarantee. There is always the possibility that your assessment can be wrong and you will end up violated. Some gay men aren't willing to take this risk because violation of trust feels psychologically analogous to annihilation. Unfortunately, no risk, no genuine intimacy. Betrayal is certainly horrific but not annihilative. We will thus explore how to broaden tolerance of this risk.

Physical Expectations

Another realm of obstacles that interferes with meeting viable partners is physical expectations. America is terribly youth and beauty oriented, and gay men are no less so. Indeed, the images we revel in do not describe the vast majority of us. Not all of us are young, have ten-inch penises, and are white. Many of us try to live up to these images, which for the majority of us is impossible. We then become self-rejecting and believe we don't "measure up." This kind of thinking is exceedingly problematic because it's likely to bring about the rejections we most fear. A man who feels physically unattractive is apt to carry himself in a way that communicates "unacceptability."

Physical expectations also work destructively in reverse. We reject men because they don't fit into certain narrowly defined categories. They must have a beard, or be six feet tall, or under age thirty-seven. This is evident in personal ads. Certainly no one should try to force himself to feel physically attracted to someone he isn't. On the other hand, being into only a certain type can be a straightjacket that fosters lost opportunities.

Age

> If you are an old gay man out cruising for sex, you are considered lascivious.
>
> Barney, forty-five
> Bus Driver, New York City

Gay men who are considered elderly are ignored by the community.

Robert, forty-seven
Grocery Store Manager, Portland, Oregon

I mentioned age in the previous paragraph, but this is an issue that deserves special attention. In a word, we are very intolerable of aging. Tired old queens and old trolls are terms common to all of us. In San Francisco, there is a bar frequented by older men. It has many windows through which you can see the customers. It has garnered a nickname: "The Glass Coffin." Although this may cause you to laugh, it belies an attitude that will comeback and bite all of us in the ass as we grow older.

Unfortunately, problems with accepting this fact of existence have many virulent manifestations in the dating arena. Some men will not go out with a person over a certain age and will therefore miss potential opportunities. Some men will lie about how old they are and do everything to look younger, sometimes looking ridiculous, frankly. Starting off with self-rejection and lies is an ideal way to doom any potential union. Still another way ageism interferes with the courting process is through development of interest only in much younger men than themselves. This is frequently a psychological attempt to deny that one is growing older. Certainly, a relationship between and a younger and older man can work. Such a bond is not necessarily cause for concern. However, *when abhorrence of aging on the part of the older man is the salient reason that the two are together, there's much to be concerned about.* Often such a union has little emotional connection and a strong monetary and power dynamic. The older man uses money to buy himself some semblance of relatedness and control. A relationship based on money and asymmetrical power cannot replace what real love and intimacy born from love can provide.

This arrangement is not beneficial to the younger man either. Being "taken care of" robs him of the opportunity to grow. It paints a bleak picture of what he has to look forward to as he matures. If he's financially dependent, he's also not free.

This is a lose/lose situation, and a foreclosure to finding a *real* life partner for both men.

Not Ready

Many men who consciously say they want a relationship are not really able to be in one—not *never,* but at a particular time because of a variety of reasons.

Some guys want the security of having a lover but are not ready to settle down and fall in love with one person. They want to play the field, and there's nothing wrong with that. The problem arises when a need for security causes them to ignore the fact that they don't want to settle down.

You may be involved in a career change or have so many work pressures that you literally do not have time for a relationship. A relationship involves a serious time commitment and you must have that time to give.

You may have recently uncoupled, and have not had enough emotional distance from your previous relationship to get involved again. Rebounding is not falling in love but *reacting* to the loss of another. A period of time without a partner is necessary before you can get involved in another serious relationship.

Still another reason may be that you are struggling with emotional problems and believe or hope that a lover will somehow deliver you from your pain. You have to first resolve those problems. A lover can enhance your life, but he is unable to give you one.

Unrealistic notions of what is involved in a relationship can also be an obstacle. Hollywood fantasy is embedded in our culture and some of us really lose perspective when it comes to love. You will thus be disappointed with any man you find and not be able to get into a relationship until your expectations become more aligned with reality.

Desperate

Sometimes you can desire a relationship too much and, as a result, prevent it from happening.

Some men are constantly on the lookout. Finding a man becomes their goal in life. Almost every situation is assessed for the potential it offers to find a partner. Although almost any situation can bring people together, being frenzied can communicate an urgency and anxiety that will push others away.

Acting desperate communicates to others that you are not someone to be involved with, no matter what strengths you actually possess. It gives others the impression that something is seriously not OK with you.

We will explore how to avoid becoming "desperate" and how to relax even in anxiety-producing situations.

Fear of Rejection

No one rejoices in being rejected. However, some men are so terrified of this that they never approach others. Sometimes they can't even notice or believe that others are interested in them. Obviously, this could cause you to miss out on meeting a life partner.

Fear of rejection can cause social paralysis. Since the first contact is the means by which any possible relationship begins, this can be a considerable problem.

Rejection fear can be related to problems with social skills. If you are not comfortable with being outgoing and meeting new people or if you have difficulty starting or maintaining a conversation, it's likely to be more difficult for you to approach and/or be with others.

Low self-esteem is often associated with fear of rejection. If you're not happy with who you are, rejection fear can be very powerful because the rejection, in your mind, is a confirmation of the negative feelings you have about yourself.

Interestingly, rejection fear, similar to many fears, is based on irrational thinking. It creates a lot of noise, brings about distress, and yet the heart of this angst has no basis in reality. The word "rejection" makes no sense because a stranger has no legitimacy to "reject" you. We will analyze this problem in depth in a later chapter and discuss strategies to overcome it.

If any or all of these issues describe your problems with finding a real life partner, you've come to the right place. You can discover how you sabotage relationships before they begin, then learn how to stop doing so. But there are still other challenges, including the question of how to identify a potential Mr. Right. You have to know what a real life partner is if you want to find him.

What characteristics are found in people serious about a long-term commitment? What are the qualities *you* need? What are the qualities you don't need but find attractive, to your detriment? How is emotional maturity defined? How do men in viable relationships deal with anxiety and intimacy? The answers to these and other questions will give you a clear outline of the kind of man you need to find.

Understanding what a real life partner is, and using your assessment ability to identify such a man, is the subject of the next chapter.

Chapter 2

What Is a Real Life Partner?

Sheldon is a handsome Jewish man raised in Brighton Beach, Brooklyn. At thirty-six, he is a high-powered lawyer with a flare for expensive clothes, classy cars, and luxurious living. He is also bright, well spoken, and worldly. He emanates social grace and is often the center of attention at social gatherings. It was at a Manhattan party that Jensen, a forty-eight-year-old journalist, met him. He was struck by Sheldon's humorous take on the Monica Lewinsky affair as he spoke to a group of people. The fellow guests were laughing rather loudly as he proclaimed that Linda Tripp was really Newt Gingrich wearing bad makeup and a wig made out of a horse's ass. Jensen joined in the laughter and noticed that Sheldon was looking at him.

They began to speak and Jensen found him very appealing. He seemed to have many interests and was well spoken as he described his life. He had a good job, was ambitious, and, most important, was single. Jensen, who had not been in a relationship for over five years, heard bells go off. Sheldon seemed to have the qualities he was looking for. They exchanged numbers and had their first date a few days later.

Their relationship became intense rather quickly. They spoke on the phone often and saw each other a least a few times during the week. Within about two months they both agreed to date each other exclusively and to have a monogamous sexual relationship.

At the end of six months, however, Jensen had become considerably frustrated and disillusioned. When he'd speak to Sheldon after a hard day at work, Sheldon had little interest or concern about how he felt. He almost seemed impatient and distracted as Jensen spoke and before long launched into a monologue about *his* day at work.

When Jensen was off on assignment, he missed Sheldon and told him so. Sheldon had no such feelings and in fact said that he thought it was a good idea for them to have time apart.

Often Sheldon was not home when Jensen called, and it would take him days before he'd return the call. This annoyed Jensen, but Sheldon refused to make any changes.

Sheldon had many "friends" but he never told Jensen much about who these people were. In fact, he rarely mentioned a name, and Jensen sarcastically joked that Sheldon knew many people with the name "Friend."

Sheldon was liberal with the truth. On more than one occasion he told Jensen stories that were grandiose. He had met this famous person, or he had been "begged" to attend this fancy party, or people regarded him as one of the smartest attorneys in the country—"smarter than Johnny Cochran." Ironically, Jensen wanted to love *him,* not the accomplishments he claimed to have achieved. Sheldon rarely shared what was truly important to him. He talked of his travels, his many experiences, and his great successes, but he hardly ever addressed what was inside of him. This made Jensen feel that he did not have a sense of who Sheldon was. It made him feel distant when he wanted to feel close.

Jensen hinted about his concerns, but Sheldon didn't seem to hear him. Eventually Jensen confronted him. He did not want to end the relationship but hoped that Sheldon would change. Sheldon seemed miffed by the fact that Jensen brought these issues up, but denied that it bothered him. In fact, he thought that Jensen may have been on to something and said he would like to think about it.

And that was the end of their relationship.

Jensen called Sheldon a few times after that, but his calls were never returned. When they finally ran into each other on the street, Sheldon behaved as if nothing had happened—indeed, as if their relationship had never happened! Jensen asked why he had not heard from him, and Sheldon said that he had been quite busy. He wished him a good day and then walked away. Jensen had by now concluded that Sheldon was not the man he had been looking for. Frustrated that he had fooled himself, but in a sense relieved that he was not longer trying to make Sheldon what he was not, he resolved to be more vigilant the next time around.

"Paper" versus Real Partner

This story is an example of how someone may appear to be good "husband material" only to demonstrate the opposite as the relationship is lived.

Being smart and funny and accomplished are real qualities and may be what first attracts you to a potential partner. But they are only a small fraction of what creates "relationship viability." By themselves they will do very little because they have nothing to do with the heart of what keeps people in love.

A real relationship means many things. At the core of such a creation is deep intimacy and sharing. There is communication and safety in feeling that you can communicate what you want and need. There is trust and honesty. There is a sense that your partner is there for you and will continue to be there for you. There is a belief in bilateral responsibility. There is an understanding that problems and difficult times will occur, but also a conviction that those challenges can be surmounted and transcended.

None of this is easy to achieve. It takes time and loads of work. But two men have to possess the personality characteristics to recognize this and buy into it, and have the motivation to do the work to make it happen.

Obviously, you are not going to be able to fully assess this when you first meet a guy. Most of us are on "good behavior" in the very early stages of courtship. In a relatively short time, however, you will be able to see the signs of whether a possible real relationship is there or not. You simply need to be looking for them.

Although we don't know what was going through Sheldon's mind, his behavior clearly demonstrated a dearth of these important qualities. He did not communicate well. He was not supportive. He did not share who he was in any meaningful way. He did not take responsibility for any problems. He was dishonest. He didn't even know how to end the relationship like a grown-up.

Perhaps Sheldon really wanted to be honest and supportive and open, but for some reasons could not demonstrate this in his behavior. Maybe he had been betrayed by a former lover and had difficulty with trust. Perhaps he had self-esteem difficulties and felt he needed to project only a "successful image." That could be true or not, but the bottom line is that he was *not* doing what he needed to do. It was not Jensen's responsibility to mind read and figure out what was really going on, or to change Sheldon. Likewise, it will not be yours when you meet someone. Your potential partner is an adult, and he should come with batteries included. If your man lacks these material qualities, it is unlikely that he will turn out to be a real life partner.

Let's take a closer look at these important qualities and others that are requisite for a viable relationship. I will break this into two categories: those that are universally essential, and those that are specifically required by you. I will start with the universal traits. I consider these essential because without them intimacy, the cornerstone of a real relationship, is unable to thrive. Of course, what you require is no less essential, but it's personally vital. Please keep in mind that although I describe this from the vantage of assessing a potential mate, it must first and foremost exist within yourself. Your assessment has to start with *yourself.*

Wanting a Relationship

Many of us freely talk about wanting to be in love. That does not automatically translate into desiring a life partner.

Love in itself is a very loosely used term. What comes to mind often is the romance involved—candlelit dinners, walks in the park, visits to exotic places, and so on. However, how many of us envision changing a dying lover's diaper, or think of dealing with money, or friends of yours he doesn't like, or mundane day-to-day life? Real love and a union conceived from that love involves all this and much more. It's imperative to think this through and be clear that someone you meet sees love in this same manner. Having excitement with someone you have just met is terribly valuable in itself. If you want him there after the music stops, you have to know if he wants to be there as well. Talking about this directly as the days and weeks pass is one way to gauge this. Some men will be up-front that they are not interested in a relationship and simply want to have fun. There is nothing wrong with that and you should accept that at face value. Some of us run into trouble when we think "he really doesn't mean that" or "if he just found the right guy"—meaning yourself—he would change his mind. Even if he is truly ambivalent, his ambivalence is warning enough. Until he has resolved this ambivalence he's not ready for a relationship.

Some men *do* say they want a life partner but demonstrate behavior to the contrary. Behavior has more weight than words. How does he conduct himself when you are not doing anything particularly special—when you are just "together"? How does he handle frustration, conflict, boredom, and boundaries? Is he fair, respectful, and sensitive to your feelings? This is part of the "stuff" of a long-term relationship. If it's not there in the beginning, don't expect it to be there later on.

Letting Go of the Single Life

There is certainly some loneliness and frustration in being single. There is less security, less of an anchor in life, less of the high you get from sharing. On the other hand, there are advantages. Being unattached means you don't have to answer to anyone. You can do what you want, whenever you want, with whomever. You have no responsibility, emotionally or otherwise, to anyone.

In a sense, being single is having the utmost in personal freedom.

Being unattached also lets you revel in fantasy about your Prince Charming. Although having a real lover can be magnificent, it can never match fantasy. Letting go of being single means you must let go of that fantasy. Some gay men don't want to give that up.

Many men who say they want a relationship really want to put an end to the discomfort of being unattached, *but they don't want to let go of the benefits.* That's similar to diving into the ocean and expecting to remain dry. It's an impossibility. There is a great deal that you can get from being in love, but you also have to give. Part of that "give" is realizing that there is someone else to consider, that the level of freedom you have in a relationship never matches what you have when you're alone.

Once again, discussing this openly and observing behavior is a way to assess what is happening. Compromise is a primary component of any viable relationship, and a man who resists finding the middle ground through any hint of reduced freedom is telling you something. A further way to consider this is to look at the role that the social scene plays in one's life. A man who has a great affinity for clubs and bars, and wants to socialize primarily in those environments may be demonstrating difficulty giving up the role of an unattached gay man. This is certainly not to say you can't go out dancing or enjoy each other in these kinds of places. It doesn't even mean that you and he can't still go to these places alone at times. When these spots become or remain the focal point of life, you should be concerned.

One thought about an open sexual relationship: there are probably as many combinations of sexual arrangements as there are gay male couples. Although some men prefer clear-cut monogamy, many others agree to outside sexual relationships under particular conditions (only on Wednesdays, when out of town, only with strangers, never at home, and so on). Although I believe the decision about monogamy versus open is not about "right" or "wrong"—it's about what is comfortable for both men in a particular couple—I do question having an open relationship in the early weeks and months as you are trying to develop a serious relationship. Not only can this cause insecurity, but it may also be a way to avoid leaving the single life. A union should never mean abdication of self, and good relationships afford an enormous amount of personal freedom. Such relationships give you the best of both worlds—love, intimacy, and freedom and support for individuation. However, being in a relationship is not being single and there is no getting around that fact.

Emotional Maturity

Real relationships are not for kids. I don't mean this in the chronological sense necessarily, although being very young makes it unlikely that you're ready for the demands of partnership.

I am referring to grown-up gay men (and straight men for that matter) who behave, think, and feel, to a large degree, like adolescents. Some of these characteristics include:

- being in significant transition, emotionally and socially (mood swings, unsure of where to live, living on a friend's couch, unclear about work/career, etc.)
- confusion about wants, needs, and goals
- having no goals
- impulsivity
- not calling back, not showing up, not telling the truth, being a flake
- self-centeredness; lack of empathy for others
- difficulty or inability to discuss feelings, concerns, desires, discomforts, etc.
- preoccupation with physical and sexual attributes of others
- preoccupation with physical and sexual attributes of self
- not taking responsibility for one's decisions and actions
- "shallow" kinds of interests "I know only about hair—don't talk to me about politics"

Obviously, someone who has all or even a few of these characteristics is not able to negotiate an adult relationship. If this is what you find, I suggest that you start running. People do change and grow up, but it's not your job to wait around for them.

And some men never grow up.

As you are reading this, you may be saying to yourself, "Oh God, I know so many gay men like that." Or you may wonder, "Is this me?"

I do believe that *some* gay men have problems with growing up and live in a limbo land of unending adolescence. Some mental health clinicians have theorized that this is related to the denial of normal adolescence in our homophobic culture. Because many gay men were in the closet as teenagers and missed the typical experience of adolescence, they are forever trying to acquire that experience. Put simply, they are trying to make up for lost time.

Whether or not some gay men actually do fit into this characterization, the point is that many gay men do not. The belief that gay men in general are emotionally immature is a homophobic conceptualization with no empirical evidence to support it. Unfortunately, many in our community accept this stereotype. This can narrow your vision and cause you to believe that this is what gay men are all about, that this is all you can hope for. It can also serve to maintain behavior in concordance with this stereotype. You may thus act flaky without realizing that you are a living out a self-fulfilling prophecy.

Trust and Support

A life partner provides a form of intimacy that exists nowhere else in your life. You experience a feeling of depth and meaning that is profound and unequaled. In this union, your lover provides immeasurable emotional grounding. He knows the *authentic you,* and he embraces and accepts that person. You are free to be the jubilant and cheerless individual, the valiant man and terrified boy, the compassionate soul and mean-spirited human. It's not that your lover won't complain and criticize and disappoint and be human also, but he has a fundamental positive regard for you that creates a sense of safety and backing which is profoundly life enhancing.

To experience this feeling, a high level of trust must exist. In a sense, you are trusting this individual with a significant component of your emotional safety. You have to know that he is ultimately on your side and that he won't turn his knowledge of your vulnerabilities against you.

Your lover must behave in a trustworthy manner that is visible to you. He has to be open so that you feel you know who he really is. There must also be a sense of communication. You have to feel that he understands what you are talking about and that you know where he is coming from.

Even in early dating, you can see if this component is there. Does he seem straightforward, or does he seem to talk in riddles? In your gut do you feel that he is telling you the truth, or is there doubt? True, if you have deep-seated problems with trust any man will seem suspect. On the other hand, instinctual feelings often give us lots of information. In his book, *The Gift of Fear: Survival Signals That Protect Us from Violence,* Gavin De Becker describes how trusting instinct can save your life. Often "instinct" means you are being communicated information that you are not consciously aware of. It's important to trust those communications. Does he seem supportive? Does he understand and care about your difficulties?

Tolerating Emotional Vulnerability
(or Getting Over That Man Stuff)

Being in love is scary for many reasons. It implies a certain amount of responsibility, curtailment of freedom, and the need to consider another human being in all the material decisions of your life. Perhaps the scariest part, however, is what it does to your psyche.

If you are in love with your partner, you have in a sense handed over some of your peace of mind to this man. His actions *do* affect you. The greatest impact he could make involves leaving you. I am not referring only to breaking up—he could die.

Love thus means emotional vulnerability. It means the potential to be hurt very badly due to the actions of, or what happens to, another. It means *not* having control.

As men we are socialized into denying emotional vulnerability. We plan. We arrange. We don't want to cry, be frightened, be unsure, be off balance, be terrified, be shocked, or have our hearts broken.

Of course, a man who attempts to live this way is not suitable for a viable relationship. Luckily, many of us are able to transcend this toxic conditioning. We are able to talk about what hurts. We recognize and accept our fears, our shortcomings. We admit that we don't always have all the answers.

If you pay attention, your potential partner will give you loads of information about his ability to tolerate emotional vulnerability. Is he able to cry? Is he able to cry in your presence? Is he aware of/sensitive to your feelings, his own, and those of others? Can he be spontaneous? How does he deal with uncertainty, confusion, being wrong, and danger? How does he handle frustration, surprises, sadness, loss, and fear? Acknowledging his humanity likely means he can tolerate emotional vulnerability.

Anxiety and Intimacy

As the days turn into weeks and months, you should be getting emotionally closer; your relationship indeed transforms. You may now use a different name—you are no longer just "dating" but you are "boyfriends." You have met some of his friends and he has met yours. Perhaps you have both decided that you will not see and/or not have sex with others. Each of us does this is our own individual way, but some form of intimacy begins to develop.

As I mentioned previously, many gay men become terrified about this and run for the hills. Although this is understandable, it's not a good sign if your new man starts to run. Intimacy is scary, and two men will have to talk about it as it happens. Distancing behavior in lieu of talking is troublesome because the chance to find a solution is minimized. Distancing can take many forms: being together feels awkward; your new guy finds reasons to avoid you; he gets inexplicably irritated after a night together; "out of the blue" he wants to see others, etc.

A real life partner needs to tolerate anxiety. If you are going to have a long-term relationship there will be many scary days. Anxiety is part of life, and the longer you are together the more likely you will experience this as a couple. Tolerating anxiety means not being overwhelmed by it. You recognize what it is, deal with it, and move on. "Dealing" means *talking* and finding a solution. *Behaving,* in lieu of talking, rarely resolves anything.

Your Personal Requirements

All of us are terribly unique creatures. Although society molds us to share numerous common values, what is personally gratifying or what is most significant is often particular to the individual. Thus, your boyfriend being employed may be important to you, but his concern that you skipped lunch or his readiness to drive you home when you work late is what really creates the fabric of your love.

Passion is a very private, idiosyncratic, behind-closed-doors phenomenon. You may fantasize about a relationship with Brad Pitt, but if you were with him and he wasn't able to touch what's inside, your relationship wouldn't work. He wouldn't be a real life partner for you.

When looking for a real life partner, it's vital both to know your personal needs and to acknowledge their legitimacy. Sometimes we feel that our personal requirements are too strange and/or unattainable and that we should be able to live without them. Sometimes they *are* unrealistic—they are derived from old wounds, such as needing your lover to be the parent you never had. But often that's not the case—it's simply what you need and *should be able to attain*. If you want your man to call you occasionally during the day just to tell you he's thinking about you, or if you like a man who is unassuming or a homebody or who is turned on by stargazing and mountain lakes, then this is the man you should be looking for.

If you have good insight about yourself, you are ahead of the game. Whatever your situation is, you should very systematically endeavor to determine what you are looking for.

Take some time for yourself when it is quiet and you are not distracted. I recommend getting up early when it's quiet outside. When you first wake up, your mind may also be quiet and more open to introspection.

Brainstorm and free-flow write what you need from a life partner. *Don't* do this on a piece of scrap paper that you may lose or not value. Invest in a nice journal.

Do this for a few mornings. Try avoiding all inhibitions and judgments. Let all the characteristics you want in the man who is going to be your life partner pour out.

After you have done this for a few days, you are ready to go back to it with a critical eye. Which of these characteristics are absolutely necessary for you? Don't worry if you find many. Don't assume "I am so high maintenance, no guy is going to be able to meet these requirements." If this is really what you need (assuming they are realistic which will be addressed shortly), you should go for it. Remember, you're not purchasing a used car that you plan to junk in a year. The man you find will be the person with whom you want to share your dreams, plans, and soul. If it will take a long time, so be it.

And one caution about time and haste. Many of us, no matter what our age, are caught up in the "911 school of finding a boyfriend." As Diana Ross sang long ago, "You Can't Hurry Love."* If you have many needs and it will take a good deal of time to find a man who will

---

*From the song "You Can't Hurry Love," words and music by Eddie Holland, Lamont Dozier, and Brian Holland, Stone Agate Music Corporation, 1965. Bestselling record in 1966 by The Supremes (Motown). *Source: Popular Music 1920-1979,* Volume 3, Nat Shapiro and Bruce Pollack, editors. Gale Research Company, Detroit, Michigan, 1985.

meet those needs, you simply have to take the time. If you find some-one who is wrong, you will be *wasting* a great deal of time by being miserable, having to go through a breakup, and then grieving loss be-fore you can move on. Respecting your needs may be frustrating as another Saturday night passes by, but the time you are taking is not a waste. It's an endeavor in honoring yourself and teaching you about what is OK and not OK for you. It also increases your chances for finding a viable relationship.

After you have clarified what is absolutely necessary, determine which characteristics are *desired* and rate them on a scale from one to three (three being most desired and one being least). Although these characteristics are not "mandatory," they are still important to you and you should be aware of them when you are out looking.

These exercises should give you a fairly good idea of what you need. This is not to say you can't come back and revise your list—in fact, it's likely you will make some changes as time passes. The point is that you are creating a tool that helps you clarify what you need in a partner as opposed to flying blind. It also helps you clarify what is nonessential for you in a relationship, so you can move on before you waste time and create unnecessary misery.

Realistic and Unrealistic

Unfortunately, no magic formula can definitively tell you what is reasonable and unreasonable to expect from a partner. I say "unfortu-nately" because if you err either way, you suffer loss. Believing you can't obtain what is in fact obtainable limits your happiness; waiting around for nothing less than perfection means you'll have a very long wait.

Having good judgment, insight, and adequate self-esteem are your best tools. They enable you to separate fantasy from reality, avoid short-changing yourself, and further clarify what you can expect by knowing what you are able to give.

In general, the unique traits you admire, the stuff that electrifies your life and creates special meaning and joy, are likely to be reason-able expectations from a partner. The following lists but a few exam-ples of what these traits might look like.

You want a man who:

- can say "I love you"
- is sexually compatible with you

- is confident
- is humble and unassuming
- can admit to being frightened and unsure
- is comfortable with sex
- has a social conscious
- is funny, makes you laugh
- is supportive
- likes your family
- can easily express emotions
- gets along with your friends
- enjoys a good party or club
- prefers more often to avoid parties and be home with you
- has friends and a life separate from you
- likes candlelit dinners
- is playful
- is romantic
- likes traveling with you
- rarely feels embarrassed
- is quiet and reserved
- is very intelligent
- craves excitement like hang gliding and skydiving
- does not engage in behavior that is dangerous and scary
- likes to occasionally drink alcohol/use recreational drugs
- drinks little or not at all; doesn't use any recreational drugs
- occasionally gives you a midday "I love you call" for no apparent reason
- occasionally buys you a shirt or some thing else for no apparent reason
- overcame major obstacles in his life
- is generally able to "be there" when you need him
- wants to share a home and pets with you
- is socially and emotionally mature
- has a cute smile, a cute voice
- has few resentments of people and life
- is creative and wild in bed
- thinks about work only during work hours
- makes you and the relationship his number-one priority

Unreasonable expectations generally mean they are not healthy desires and not realistic. Even if a lover could somehow satisfy such requirements, they would be an impediment to your growth, his growth, and the development of your relationship. Examples of this include desiring a lover who will:

- take away your depression
- give you confidence
- take away your fear of being alone
- provide you with adequate self-esteem
- guarantee he will never leave you
- take away your anxieties
- always anticipate your needs
- meet all of your needs
- be the only important person in your life
- consider you the only important person in his life
- always put you before everyone else in his life
- make you feel financially secure (he could pay your way, but it's doubtful you will *feel* secure)
- make you trust
- take away your anger and bitterness
- heal the wounds of your childhood
- be the parent, psychologically, that you needed but never had
- stop your chemical/alcohol/sex/etc. addictions
- put your out-of-control life back in control
- enable you to negotiate the difficulties of life
- be the answer to all of your prayers
- make you happy

Sex and Beauty

An enjoyable physical relationship is not only a reasonable expectation but also necessary. It's difficult for a partnership to thrive with sexual discontent.

A real life partner is about being with a man whom you find physically and sexually alluring. It's about your blood raging when you anticipate sex with him. It's about enjoying his physical being. But it's not about fondling the perfect dick owned by the perfect body in an unending fantasy of flawless carnal pleasure. Real life partners exist in real life.

Countless gay men seeking love also want the former, however.

Sorry to say it doesn't work that way.

Not only is most of the world *not* made up of porno gods, *but hot sex and physical satisfaction are not predicated by bodily perfection.* You and your lover may never be in a Ralph Lauren commercial but can still set yourselves and the world ablaze.

Furthermore, physicality is only a piece of the puzzle. There is much more to love and romance, and when we weigh in so heavily on the physical, we end up falling, face first, into cow shit. Thinking with your penis can make the wrong guy seem right until it gets so bad that there's no more room for denial. More fundamentally, our emphasis on the physical, which is often so out of line with reality, makes us pass up viable partners and, even worse, erodes our self-esteem.

Chapter 3 examines reverence for the body and how this interferes with finding a man. We're also going to visit ageism, which is a particularly destructive aspect of this preoccupation.

Obsession with beauty and youth will confine your life. You can change your outlook and create opportunities in place of limitations.

Chapter 3

The Gay Culture of Pretty:
How to Live with the Face You Have

The real terrible thing about this physical stuff is the psychological idea, "I am lovable if I'm beautiful." . . . Our idea of what makes us valuable and lovable narrows to such a terrible degree.

Thomas Moon, MFT
Private Practice, San Francisco, California

There's not a damn thing that you can do about it except a lot of plastic surgery or other crazy stuff, which isn't really going to do anything to your spirit.

Brian Wolfe, MFT
Private Practice, San Francisco, California

On New Year's Eve 1999, I accompanied some friends to a bar that featured male dancers. One of the performers was an extremely beautiful young man. I watched in awe as he slowly and methodically progressed to virtual nudity. Many other men were enraptured with him, and some stuffed dollar bills into what was left of his skimpy clothing. On the stage towering above the crowd, with hordes of hungry men gawking and paying for his beauty, he epitomized the physicality so many gay men desire. Such appeal generated incredible sexual tension.

I certainly enjoyed watching him, but I also have to admit that I felt some discomfort. I knew I looked nothing like him, that I could never measure up, even if I were twenty years younger. I mused with more than a tinge of envy that he was terribly fortunate to be young and beautiful and *so* hot.

The lover of a friend of mine once remarked how I could never be a dancer in this bar. "People would clear out," he joked. I was not amused at the time, and I am not laughing now. Although I never intended to pursue a new vocation, I didn't like to think of myself as "clearing a place out." What the hell is wrong with me? I wondered, am I not good-looking enough? Am I too old? Why was my friend involved with such a jerk?

These thoughts flooded my mind. I was feeling a little out of sorts. Not a great way to begin a new year.

It arrived, nevertheless, along with a moment of truth.

At the strike of midnight this fellow was still dancing. But now a very changed picture emerged. As others and I embraced, as friends and strangers wished one another good tidings, as lovers kissed, and as popping and flowing champagne celebrated a sense of community, this man continued to dance. *All by himself. Little attention was being paid to him. He was sharing the moment with no one.*

Of course, I knew nothing about his situation. Maybe he had many friends and just had to work that night. Conceivably he had a lover at home. I certainly wasn't uninfluenced by my earlier feelings of jealousy. Perhaps I wanted to see him in a negative light.

Nevertheless, he looked quite isolated and certainly unimportant to the same people who only moments earlier were salivating over him.

I saw in this a contrast between the value of physical beauty and the worth of human connection. The former seemed like an optical illusion, the latter, something of immeasurable importance.

I also derived an important lesson that is applicable to the business of looking for a life partner: being gorgeous has little to do with finding him.

Physical beauty certainly does have its place. It is part of sexual attraction, and sexual feelings are terribly powerful. Physical attractiveness also holds real influence in the world at large. If they think you are cute, people will give you attention, which is ego gratifying. It can also bestow opportunities. An attractive person may get a job, for example, that a less attractive one, although equally qualified, may not be offered.

We get into trouble, however, when we give looks more significance than they really have; we get into real trouble when this factors heavily in seeking a partner.

Sex

Sex is very important, but *physical beauty is often confused with sexual attraction*. They are not the same. Although sexual attraction *is* requisite for a relationship to be workable, your boyfriend doesn't have to be beautiful for that to happen. You don't have to be beautiful either. No one has to meet a fantasy standard of perfection that many in the gay community demand without even realizing it.

The gay press is rife with images that have little to do with real life. If you were a visitor from Mars and were exposed only to those images, you'd think that all gay men were white, under thirty, had big muscles, enormous penises, and engaged in sex incessantly. Of course, you don't have to be from Mars to be influenced by that kind of propaganda. The media has a very powerful effect on our thinking, often on a subconscious level. The fantasy images that are disseminated become the standard by which you and a prospective partner are measured.

Obviously, there are serious problems with this. You may simply not look like those pictures—and nothing you can do will ever make you look that way. If you can't feel good unless you do, you will spend lots of time feeling miserable. If you demand physical perfection from a prospective mate, you'll be treading the same dubious path. The men you meet will fall short of your ideal beauty and you will reject them.

It's not that beautiful men don't exist and that you will never encounter one, but if that is *all* that is acceptable to you, you are seriously limiting your options.

The good news is that you don't need any of this in either yourself or someone else to have wonderful sex.

Sexual desire and enjoyment come from many sources, not the least of which is the personality of a person. If you don't believe me, answer this question: Did you ever find yourself saying "he looked gorgeous until he opened his mouth"? Did you ever spend hours in hot pursuit of a guy only to wonder what on earth possessed you after you spent the night with him? Who a person is and what that means to you will have an impact on your sexual feelings for him. Indeed, developing loving feelings can help produce sexual ones. Moreover, your loving feelings may expand your perception of what you consider beautiful. Thus, the not-so-gorgeous stranger may look a lot prettier once you get to know him.

Another determinant of sexual excitement is sexual compatibility. Have you ever gone to bed with a gorgeous guy only to discover that he was a dud? What a person does sexually, and how he does it, is very important. You can't tell that from staring at him from across the room (hankies and all that other stuff aside!).

To give yourself the opportunity to find sexual compatibility, you have to be open to men who may not be particularly beautiful and forgive yourself for the same.

This doesn't mean that you can't pursue men who do appear to fit into your fantasy or that you should look for those who are truly unappealing to you. It simply means being more flexible. Be realistic about the role beauty will have at the end of the day in terms of a relationship, and know that sexual enjoyment is multidimensional.

Growing Older: A Very Complex Topic

There's no avoiding the fact that beauty is associated with youth. Although this is certainly a pervasive American "value," it is assuredly a gay male issue.

The topic of ageism in the gay community is worthy of many books. Certainly no attempt to exhaustively examine this problem is being made here. However, I do believe a few comments are warranted.

Ageism creates innumerable problems for all of us. It produces psychological difficulties and makes life a lot harder to enjoy. It creates a distaste for birthdays and a concern that we are no longer acceptable. It causes us to think and behave with disdain toward those who are older. All of this is individually and collectively destructive. Furthermore, it negatively impacts the chances of creating a viable relationship.

Ageism is mutigenerationally damaging. Young gay men, sometimes men even in their twenties, worry that they are too old and engage in behavior to hide and deny their real age. This includes lying about one's age, undergoing cosmetic surgery, and feeling inferior to, and jealous of, those who are actually younger. Young gay men may see no future in getting older and have fatalistic feelings about life in general.

Older gay men may feel they are no longer attractive. This creates substantial impediments to meeting people. Avoidance of social situations is not the only way this can manifest. If you don't like yourself because of how old you are, it's going to be hard for others to like you. You may project self-rejection while engaging with another, and *this can cause disinterest by that person in you.* Self-rejection can be communicated unconsciously, and the other person may decide he'd rather not proceed without even realizing why.

Obsession with Youth

Ageism can contribute to obsessively searching for partners substantially younger that oneself. Revulsion regarding one's advancing age, rather than a simple preference, is at the root of such behavior. It's a way to psychologically deny one's age. Denial in this manner can only be damaging.

Searching for a real life partner while pursuing youth can resemble a rat running on a treadmill. You're not dealing in reality and therefore are unlikely to find anything real. Sadly, the purpose of youth pursuit is to keep yourself young, not to fall in love with another adult.

Focusing on youth short of obsession is still tricky. Potential partners are likely to be screened out while the wrong people are sought after. Although a large variance in age can exist in viable relationships, it presents significant challenges to the men in those unions. Large variance in age means vastly different life experiences, dissimilar developmental challenges, and different needs. If you are hooked on youth it may be difficult to find a partner who can meet your emotional, intellectual, and spiritual requirements. Someone who is older may understand you better, have the kind of emotional maturity you expect and need, and be there for you in a way that a younger man simply cannot. Of course there are immature older men and young men who are grown-up beyond their years. In general, however, you simply can't expect someone who hasn't lived enough to have the vantage point of one who has. That is often an important ingredient in a workable relationship.

Lying About Your Age

Because so many of us abhor aging, we lie, at times, about how old we really are. Dishonesty is the worst way to begin any form of relationship, and this is exactly how you are beginning if you lie about how old you are.

Some men feel that if they tell the truth before they meet the person (such as chatting with someone online) or before a prospective partner gets to really know them, it will prevent them from ever having the chance to begin a relationship. Although this may be true, a potential relationship is tainted if it begins with lies. Trust and honesty are vital components of a viable relationship. They are the building blocks of real intimacy. If a relationship begins with a lie, it spews poison on the potential creation. You don't get a second chance to make a first impression, and that lie may unravel what could have been. Gay men already have a particularly difficult time with trust. Beginning a relationship with a falsehood is an effective way to do industrial-strength damage.

There is also another serious problem. If you fear a person may not want you because you are too old, if you feel he would categorically reject you based on a vital and unchangeable fact of who you are, why would you want to get to know someone like that in the first place? A healthy relationship means being accepted and loved for who you really are. Thus, aside from the trust issue, lying about your age is destructive because it is a form of self-deprecating behavior. Attempting to begin a relationship by maneuvering around an anticipated rejection relative to an unchangeable fact is ludicrous. Being able to "convince" the person later on to accept you *despite* that fact is no triumph. Even if that were to happen, you still began on the wrong foot. You told yourself in no small way that you are not OK because of your age.

Self-Esteem and Age

Any assault on self-esteem has huge costs in all aspects of life. When you don't feel good about yourself, you are likely to make decisions congruent with a negative image. Often it's subtle and unconscious, but if you feel "less than" you will create a "less than" world for yourself. This can manifest by derailing a potentially viable relationship before it starts. Aside from being "rejected," as I described previously, *you* may find a way out if your potential partner does not. You may forget to call him, lose interest, or do 1,000 other things (probably unconsciously) that will make the relationship not happen. Conversely, you will pursue those who are not good for you. Being caught up in prettiness and feeling less than because you are not pretty or young can bring this about.

One maddening aspect of a preoccupation with physical beauty is that you may never feel good enough or "safe" for very long. Beauty is a very subjective concept. When beauty becomes your focus, it may change rather abruptly relative to the environment. You may thus be only as beautiful as the last person who was physically attracted to you thought. Some men experience these ups and downs on a continuous basis. They are never sure of how they appear. This puts their self-esteem on a roller coaster and interferes with their ability to relate to others. If you feel constantly unsure that you are "good enough," it is going to be very hard for you to feel confident enough to pursue and develop a real relationship. The guy who showers you with incessant attention may help you feel good for a while, but as soon as he needs to do something else (like his laundry), you may take it personally. This can destroy a potential relationship rather quickly.

What Really "Makes" a Relationship

At the end of the day, physicality is but one aspect of being with someone you love. A real relationship is a dyad with many elements. You form a bond with someone who's developmentally and spiritually compatible. You share the journey with someone who shares your values, whom you can respect, whom you can communicate with, who can be there when you really need him. You connect with a man whom you can trust, whom you like, whom you can have fun with, who can be your friend, who can be your soul mate, whom you can love in a profoundly deep and meaningful way. This is what you should be looking for *because this is what a life partner is all about.*

Taking Action

Physical appearance, of course, does play a role in meeting others. Being clean and well groomed is important. Wear clothing you like and feel comfortable in, because that will affect how you present yourself.

But that's about where it all ends! Contrary to the popular belief that beauty is the opening ticket, your mouth really is. As long as you can talk, you can meet someone and let him know just how attractive you are. When someone short of a raving beauty approaches you, you also can listen for the gems and watch for the sparks that may be what you've longed for.

Believing you can be yourself and find a life partner, whatever you look like, how ever many years you've walked this earth, is paramount.

Strong beliefs, certainly those that are supported by cultural values, take work to change. There are many ways you can do this.

First, begin by having a conversation with yourself. Think about the logic, the evidence, or rather the lack thereof, of beauty being equated with finding love.

For example, do you know of people who are in love, who live happy fulfilled lives together, and are short of drop-dead gorgeous? How can that be if good looks are requisite for a relationship?

Do you know of people who have been together for many years? If a relationship has spanned decades, the people in them can't be youngsters. Do you know of any people like that who are still in love? If they are, how can they be in love and have wrinkles and sagging flesh? Why not go and ask them? (You don't have to say, "How do those wrinkles and sagging flesh not get in the way of your love?" Just ask them what keeps it alive!)

Do you know of beautiful lonely people? Do you know of beautiful guys who want a relationship and can't seem to find one? Have you ever met a beautiful guy but couldn't have a relationship with him because "other things" were missing? What value did his looks ultimately have?

Have you had the experience of being with a lover or close friend when he was dying? Did his physical appearance diminish your love for him? If you were *in love* with him, did you fall out of love because of what he looked like?

Although the answers to these questions are easy and obvious, it's important to view them in relation to the thoughts you have about finding a man. They underscore the dearth of logic inherent in the immense value we place on physicality.

Talk to Others

It's also important to have conversations with other gay men about this issue. Start talking with others about all the hoopla surrounding age and beauty. I'm confident you'll find many who recognize the problem and will be supportive of you in your endeavor to change your view.

You may have good friends with whom you can discuss this, or perhaps you should join a gay men's group. If there isn't one in your area, why not start one? Call it "what really makes a relationship." Who knows, it's entirely possible you could meet someone in that group!

Act the Part Despite How You Feel

Although you may not yet have new beliefs, *start acting as if you do.* I know this may feel awkward at first, but often behavior can change beliefs, not just the other way around. Thus, if you approach people with the *attitude* that you don't have to meet an arbitrary standard of physical prowess, that you are fine just being who you are, you are likely to get a positive response. That, in turn, will support the belief that you really *are* OK just being you.

Love Yourself

To help further produce this belief is to stop denying your physical core. You can start *by working on accepting yourself just as you are.* For example, if you are in your fifties, do not try to imitate styles and clothing of those worn by teenagers and men in their early twenties. Besides looking inappropriate, this behavior is an attempt to be something you are not; as such, you are telling yourself that you are not OK. The same thing goes with other physical alterations such as diets, hair replacement, plastic surgery, hair dying, etc. This is not to say that you shouldn't ever engage in any of these. What you need to know is *why* you are doing it and if it is a way to hide who you are. If you really prefer dark hair to gray, by all means dye your hair. But if it is a desperate attempt to make yourself look years younger than you are, I would think twice. The same goes for surgery to change the way you look, or diets to lose significant weight. A diet may be fine for health reasons and you may like looking thinner and feeling better physically. But if being heavy means you are *fat* and *ugly* and *unacceptable* and *disgusting, a diet can actually work to support your feelings of unacceptability.* In terms of surgery, I would think long and hard (and probably consult with a mental health professional) before I underwent something for cosmetic purposes. Again, it doesn't mean that to do this is always a mistake. The point is, be very clear as to why you want it. If you truly do not accept who you are, surgery is likely to change little about your feelings. Embracing who you really are will help produce an attitude of self-acceptance that will be communicated to the world.

Another strategy is to take a good look at yourself in the mirror and *tell yourself that you are good enough just because you exist.* This may seem odd, but consider that this says volumes about our odd culture.

We place so much emphasis on what a human being does and how he appears that we forget about the *being* part of human being. That is the true essence of human value and the basis of positive self-esteem. No combination of looks or worldly accomplishments or possessions will ever make you feel good about yourself, but you can feel good about yourself *just because you are a human being on this earth.* When you truly believe this, life becomes much easier because you don't have to *do* anything particularly special to love yourself.

It's easy to understand this when you observe an animal, such as a dog. He doesn't have to do anything particularly special for you to love him. *You love him because he's there. He has value because he's alive.*

You can do the same for yourself. Look into the mirror and say this. *There is nobody in this world that was ever or ever will be the unique me.* (Yes, even if they clone you. Your clone is still not you!) *I am precious and wonderful and special and more rare than the rarest gem. And I can never, ever be replaced.*

Say this to yourself as you are looking in the mirror no matter how awkward it makes you feel. Do this exercise a number of times a day, especially when you wake up and before you go to sleep. It may also help to find a picture of you as a child. Take a look at that kid and ask yourself: *Is he not good enough? Does he have to do something to be OK? Is that nose, those eyes, those ears, that hair, that missing front tooth not OK? Is he not anything but beautiful?*

Hopefully you'll find him perfect!

I suggest you do this as a regular exercise.

Accept Others

It's also important to embrace others who you do not consider physically beautiful. Don't immediately decline an opening from someone who doesn't meet your standard of beauty. In fact, I recommend trying to meet others who you don't find gorgeous, or who aren't your "type." There are two advantages to this. Relating to others based on the value of who they are as people, not just what they look like, will support your effort to change the beliefs about yourself. The other advantage is that you may discover that you really want to get to know that person. There are so many ways to start relationships. This is one.

Special Emphasis on Ageism

Although you may have addressed ageism in that conversation with yourself and others, do it again. Aging is a horrific taboo in our culture and in the gay community. We dread getting older and do everything we can to deny it.

Take a frank look at what this is all about for you. Age is closely related to physicality, and coming to terms with getting older will help you come to terms with accepting and loving who you are.

If you're lucky, you will get old and lose your physical loveliness before you return to dust. Not an enchanting thought, but it's a fact of life. Running from this makes it worse.

Getting older is not all bad news, however. There are actually many advantages. Many older men feel less anxious and less caught up with the highs and lows of sexuality, and are more able to appreciate the deeper aspects of being in a relationship. Age also means more experience, and some of those bad relationships may now come in handy as lessons to help you locate the *right* Mr. Right. Age sometimes produces better sexuality, because you're likely to be more experienced in how to pleasure yourself and others. Age often means better financial and career achievement. The house and dog that you'd dreamed of sharing with your partner in your early twenties may now actually happen.

Whatever age you are, it's in your best interest to have intergenerational connections. Positive images of older gay men are sorely absent, which is very destructive for all of us. It's important for the younger among us to see that life doesn't end at forty or even much beyond that. Knowing older gay men will afford you the role models you need in order to embrace the inevitable. For older gay men, contact with younger guys means inclusion and seeing the vantage point of a different generation. This builds self-esteem as it enhances growth.

If you are unable to transcend beyond looks and age, it may help to consult a therapist. Significant difficulties with accepting oneself are unlikely to change without professional help.

If you don't like yourself, it's going to be very difficult to be attractive to others. Your feelings will be communicated and people will respond negatively. Or you will reject them before they get a chance *not* to want you.

On the other hand, if you recognize the immense worth you possess distinct from any physical attributes, you will be far more attractive than mere skin and muscles.

Looking for Him "Out There"

Being comfortable with yourself will make being "out there" less scary. But the "looking for relationship arena" comes with built-in anxiety. It takes energy and fortitude to attend social situations, to put yourself on the line, to go after and not always get what you want.

Yet anxiety often has a lot more to do with what we tell ourselves than the actual challenges we face. When we feel frightened, more than likely we're telling ourselves only part of the story, the most negative, most scary, and ironically, *most unlikely* outcome. Looking for a partner does have uncertainty and is challenging, but it doesn't have to be torturous. It actually can be exciting and fun. You have the power to make it that way.

Chapter 4

Searching Anxiety:
How to Talk to Any Man You Want

I do find guys that are desperate a turn-off as it indicates to me they are not comfortable with themselves.

Warner, thirty-four
Nurse, Baltimore, Maryland

It was another Saturday night for Jonathan, a software engineer who lived in San Jose, California. As he drove north along highway 280 to San Francisco, his stomach felt queasy. He was going to attend the birthday party of his friend Romero.

He knew there would be a lot of cute of guys at the party, and he was excited and nervous. His birthday would be coming up in a month and he just didn't want to turn forty-eight with "no one." "I really should have met someone already, god damn it," he told himself as he pushed the accelerator closer to the floor. Both of his best friends, Carl in San Jose and Seymour in New York, were in relationships. In fact, Seymour and his partner Kevin just celebrated three years together and bought a one-bedroom co-op in Chelsea. "Damn it," he continued to himself. "What the hell is wrong with me? I'm pissing money. I could have a big house with someone. What do Seymour and Carl have that I don't?"

He reached the apartment in the Castro; he could feel sweat in his palms as he rang the bell. Romero welcomed him with a diva kiss on the lips and then introduced him to some of the other guests. It was crowded and teeming with hot young men. He felt his heart accelerate. "This is pay dirt," he told himself as he rushed to grab a Budweiser. The night held many possibilities and he wasn't going to let any of them pass.

Because there were so many good-looking men, he felt increasingly anxious. As he spoke with one guy, his eyes would focus on others. The other men would appear more attractive and he'd feel he should be talking to them. He'd then excuse himself and approach someone else.

The more he did this, the more anxious he became, and the more Budweisers he drank. He wanted to find the right guy and didn't want to waste time.

Before long he was drunk. He felt sexy for a while and talked at warp speed and laughed a good deal. But the evening wore on and he met no one. His veil of intoxication could not hide what was happening. The men he approached were polite but weren't interested in him. When he noticed it was midnight he became very uneasy. He then began working harder, approaching men and asking them if they would take a walk with him or give him their phone numbers. All politely refused, and he had the uncomfortable realization that he was making a fool out of himself. At 1:30 a.m. all of the guests were gone. Romero, knowing how drunk Jonathan was, insisted that he sleep over. As he lay down on his friend's couch, Jonathan felt depressed and defeated. Once again, he had met no one. Once again a Saturday night was "ruined." He wondered how long this would go on, and was then hit with a horrific thought: *he knew the answer—he would never meet anyone.* He fell into a restless sleep, resolving to stop pursuing a hopeless endeavor.

If you want something a great deal and you don't have it, it's understandable you could feel discomfort. There is a challenge before you, an uncertain outcome, and anguish in some form if your mission doesn't succeed.

If finding a partner is a major life goal, it's foolhardy to think you can pursue this without some stress. But there's a crucial difference between resolve and desperation.

Anxiety and Societal Rules

I do sometimes feel that time is running out on me to find a partner because I am getting older. My actual thoughts are, (1) oh my God, If I can't find anyone now, I will never find one; (2) I'm going to be alone for the rest of life; (3) there must be something wrong with me. All these thoughts affect my behavior profoundly. I start to act very desperately and I have no patience whatsoever. Everyone I meet I see as a potential partner. When a guy likes me and I like him, I tend to want to have a relationship with him right away, even though I don't really know him that well.

Blake, twenty-seven
Photographer, Minneapolis, Minnesota

As in the example with Blake and Jonathan, a large part of desperation is related to fear and feelings of inadequacy. Much less comes from actually being lonely and/or wanting to find love. The loneliness and desire for love is very real, but think about it this way: If you weren't on a timetable as these men were, if you believed that viable partners are "out there," if you *truly believed* that a life partner would eventually come along, if you didn't compare yourself to others who had boyfriends, if you didn't think about all the things "wrong" in you that caused you to be single, just how desperate and miserable could you be?

Unfortunately many of the irrational notions that torture us are derived from deeply ingrained precepts of our culture. A person feeling miserable during the Christmas season is an excellent example of this. During Christmas, especially on Christmas Day, you are supposed to:

- be with loved ones
- have a wonderful meal with loved ones
- be filled with love and good cheer toward others
- give lots of presents
- receive lots of gifts
- be thankful for all you have
- be blissfully happy

How can you *absolutely be happy* just because it's a sacred holiday? How can you *absolutely feel good will toward others* if you just don't feel like it on that particular day? It's wonderful if you can, but how can you command yourself to feel that way? What if you have no partner, your best friend is in Peru, and your hemorrhoids flare up?

As irrational as it sounds, being less than mirthful on Christmas can turn into an emotional crisis because *it's Christmas. People feel bad about feeling bad because you're not supposed to feel bad on Christmas!*

What a splendid way to drive yourself crazy!

What's taking place is a "societal rule"—Christmas is a time to feel happy—that millions *believe and feel compelled to follow* despite its questionable logic.

In an analogous manner, the beliefs we have about gay relationships, many of which are irrational, semiconscious, tinged with internalized homophobia, and also *unquestioned* by millions, do the same thing. *They tell us that this is the way it is and we think and behave in terms of them.* As with the previous example, they do damage to us. They injure by setting up a false picture of scarcity, limitations, time running out, and hopelessness. In such a mind-set, pursuit of a partner can assume a desperate aura.

Some of these general "gay societal rules" include:

- There is no one out there anymore.
- There was never anyone out there.
- Once you're _____ (fill in the age—likely your own!), it's too late to find a partner.
- All gay men are flighty and shallow.
- You have to be beautiful and muscular and have a big dick to have a boyfriend.
- All the quality guys are taken.
- You can't be happy without a partner.
- There is something wrong if you are single.
- You should have a boyfriend by age _____.
- It's pathetic to be looking for a boyfriend at age_____.
- All gay men just want sex.

Note that these beliefs can contradict each other. If all gay men are shallow and flighty, for example, how can all the *quality* men be taken? If *all* gay men are superficial, how was there ever any *quality* men that could be taken? And taken by whom?

These "general societal beliefs" help form personal beliefs that can make the search agonizing.

As you look for a boyfriend, you may feel desperate because you think:

- I'm on my way to ending up old and alone.
- I'm too old; my chances have passed me by.
- I will never find the kind of person that I need with so many flakes out there.
- I must appear younger than I am in order to catch anyone's eye.
- A decent guy is one in a million; if I meet someone like that I can't let him slip away.
- Finding the right man is similar to finding pie in the sky; I might as well settle with second best.
- Why did I ever leave my ex (even though I couldn't stand him!)? Now I'm out in the cold.
- It's embarrassing to be single; what's wrong with me?

- Something is inherently wrong with me; otherwise I wouldn't be alone.
- Everyone else has a partner; I'm not lovable.
- I feel very angry that this is so hard. Gay men piss me off.
- I can't stand being alone—I must find a boyfriend.
- Being single is absolutely horrible. I can't live without a partner.
- I must find a boyfriend in the next six months or sooner.
- I must be very wealthy/smart/talented/etc. or at least convince someone of that to find a man.
- Deny, lie—do whatever it takes to find a man.
- I must be constantly ready, in any situation, to meet a potential spouse.
- I should go out a lot, even when I don't feel like it, in order to find someone.
- I should go to bars, even though I don't like them. That's where all the available guys are.
- I shouldn't waste any time if I don't feel immediate sparks. There is no time to waste.
- I am a failure because I am alone.
- I am terrified to be in social situations. Everyone will know I'm alone and a loser.

If you are thinking this way, your anxiety will be quite high not only when you are in social situations, but also when you are home alone. This can produce a host of undesirable outcomes.

To begin with, you will make your experience of being single quite miserable. This can lead to more anxiety, anger, bitterness, and even clinical depression. Not exactly the makings of a fun guy or a choice catch! Furthermore, your quest to find a mate will be tinged with the cry "get me out of here." Although you may try to hide this feeling, it will be revealed. It may be communicated from a desperate look in your eyes, a need to talk fast or dominate the conversation, your posture, a premature quest for a telephone number, or a host of other behavioral manifestations. Oftentimes the person who is reading these signals is not consciously aware of what they mean, but he knows something isn't right and for some reason doesn't want to get to know you. The cry "get me out of here" says, in effect, "I am not good as I am; I am not whole. I need you to make me OK." Most psychologically healthy gay men will find this very unattractive and avoid people who act this way.

Of course, you may find someone who wants to "rescue" you, or someone else who in other ways is not appropriate for you. When you are in that kind of a frenzy, your assessment and judgment tools are not fully operational.

If you are thinking, "But I do have these thoughts—my desperation is real," you may also conclude "I can't do anything about it."

I say, "Oh, yes, you can!"

Taking Action/Challenging Beliefs

The aforementioned convictions have crucial rifts with logic and reality, but I do not ask you to accept that because I say so. As with the "connection" between beauty and finding love, you have to discover for yourself "what is" in order for it to be incorporated into your belief system. I would therefore ask you, as I did before, to look for the *evidence,* the *proof or the lack thereof.* Keep in mind that there are always grains of reality in most beliefs, no matter how otherwise distorted. The question is: can you really conclude from those "grains" any universal truths? For example, there are many gay men (as there are heterosexual fellows) who behave in an immature, irresponsible, and dishonest fashion. But where is the *evidence* that *all* or almost all gay men behave this way? If you step back from your preconceived notions and investigate this, as a scientist would, you will have serious problems finding that evidence.

When I work with clients with low self-esteem, for example, I inform them that they are going to have to find real evidence that they are failures, fools, losers, etc., in order to continue feeling crappy. If the evidence is not there and they realize that, it's going to be almost impossible for them to continue feeling bad about themselves.

When you look for the evidence of a need to be desperate, you are more likely to discover evidence of homophobia. Indeed, many of those negative ideas (but not all) are related to homophobia—societal messages that label being gay as an aberrant, inferior, hopeless, pathetic, mentally ill, criminal (I could go on) lifestyle. Despite all the changes in the last quarter of the twentieth century homophobia still exists, and most of us were exposed to the more virulent forms as children. It is in our collective psyche, and we have to work hard at exposing it and preventing it from running and ruining our lives.

There are numerous ways to accomplish this. First you must be *open* (not necessarily convinced) to the *possibility* that what you think is not the whole picture or is blatantly false. Then go look for the evidence. Again, I'm not asking you to categorically renounce what you believe. If your thoughts are assumptions, perhaps held by many but not supported by fact, you need to ask yourself if there is another way to look at those thoughts. For example, let's take a closer look at the thought from the previous list that a decent gay man is "one in a million." This doesn't seem like good odds. But ask yourself this: Are you, generally speaking, "decent?" What about your friends? What kind of gay men do you let into your inner circle? Are they empty, shallow, dishonest thieves or people who will be and have been there when you needed them? What about your friends' partners? Any of them decent? Have you even been involved with a decent lover even if it ultimately didn't work out?

My guess is that you are going to come up with a sizable number of honorable fellows. Not everyone, but more than one in a million. If that's true, how could decency out there be so rare? Are you and your circle dramatically different from the rest of the population? Unless there is a secret society of "them," there are likely many, many gay men who are quite respectable.

Being Aware of Self-Talk

Looking for the evidence means also being aware of your self-talk. What you say inside your head can have profound effects on your feelings and behavior. It's particularly important to be aware of the words you use because your mind tends to take those words literally. In the last example, your brain will comprehend the phrase one in a million to mean exactly that. Other words such as *never, always, all, totally, impossible, most, forever, horrendous,* although rarely accurate (*all* gay men lie; I've *never* met a nice man; I will *always* be alone; meeting someone today is *impossible;* being single is *horrendous,* etc.), are what your mind hears and *believes.*

Self-talk occurs at a rapid speed so it's imperative to slow it down. You can do this by reflecting on what you're telling yourself when you're having a strong feeling. For example, if you feel very happy when a friend gives you a birthday gift, listen to what you just told yourself. It may go something like this: "He's such a sweetheart. He really cares about me. How nice of him to remember my birthday."

Conversely, when you are feeling uncomfortable, make an effort to be aware of what you are telling yourself. In the previous vignette describing Jonathan's desperation at a party, we can surmise some of his self-talk: "I must meet someone tonight. I am so alone and so old and everyone else has a partner so I must meet someone. God, this place has so many beautiful men. There is no excuse not to meet someone tonight. I have to make the right choice, though. I can't waste time with the wrong guy because then the right guy might pass me by. But who is the right guy? I can't make a mistake."

Because self-talk is rapid it's usually helpful to write out what you're thinking. You may want to set up a journal with pages that have the following column headings:

- Incident
- Self-talk
- Evidence for
- Evidence against
- More balanced conclusion

Writing your thoughts out in this way can catch self-talk in action, identify your triggers, help you search for the evidence, and help you change your outlook and feelings.

In the previous example Jonathan could have written down the following:

- *Incident:* Party—lots of beautiful men
- *Self-talk:* Must meet someone tonight. I'm so old. There's no excuse if I don't meet someone at a party with so many hot guys.
- *Evidence for:* There *are* many cute guys here. That's a fact. There should be someone for me with so many guys present. I am almost forty-eight; I want to meet someone and it's time I did.
- *Evidence against:* It's only one party. There will be others. No matter how many guys are here, there has to be the right chemistry. There is no law saying I must meet someone *tonight*. Yes, I'm almost forty-eight but I'm not almost dead.

- *More balanced conclusion:* There are lots of men here and the right one could be in the crowd. But he may not be and besides *I don't have to meet someone tonight.* It would be nice to, but it wouldn't be the end of the world if I didn't. There will be other chances. The pressure is irrational and I'm causing it. So I'll let it go, calm down, and enjoy myself! As a matter of fact, I'm more likely to meet someone if I'm relaxed.

This example demonstrates how the evidence to make Jonathan miserable was really lacking, When he realized this, his thoughts and, most important, his *feelings* changed. In real life, it's not always convenient to write out your thoughts, and this one exercise would not likely have changed Jonathan's views and feelings. However, when you do this kind of exercise on a regular basis, it can have very powerful results. Doing it consistently (even though you can't do it in all situations) gets you into the habit of observing your self-talk and not taking at face value any toxic stream of words that may cross your psyche. It also enables you to determine the evidence, and, as I said earlier, if you determine that there's no reason (evidence) to feel miserable (or desperate, which is a pretty miserable feeling), it's going to be exceedingly difficult to feel that emotion.

Beliefs and Self-Talk

Jonathan's self-talk came from a number of beliefs that were ingrained long before the night of the party—the primary one being his battle with time. Although it's important to be aware of and confront caustic self-talk when in a high anxiety setting, it's most important to question beliefs and related self-talk before you are confronted with the situation. Accomplishing this when you are less nervous can better enable you to confront destructive self-talk (or even prevent it from occurring) in anxiety-provoking situations.

Jonathan had not addressed his beliefs—that time was running out for him, that everyone had boyfriends, and that he *should* have a boyfriend *by now.* As a result, he turned a potentially fun event into a life-and-death struggle. Had he experienced the evening without that toxic internal chatter, he would have had a much better chance of meeting someone. He would have been more attractive to others, would not have appeared so desperate, and would have been in a more favorable position to assess a potential mate. Jonathan's panic short-circuited his capacity for evaluation. He simply ran from one pretty face to another. He didn't give himself a chance to see what was behind the faces or to appreciate how his behavior was being evaluated.

Talking It Out

Discussing these kind of issues with nonjudgmental friends, in a gay men's support group, and/or with a professional counselor can be helpful.

"As If" Behavior—Trying on a New Persona

Still another way to deal with this is through what I call forced, "as if" behavior. I discussed this concept in relation to physical appearance. If you recall, it simply means to act as if you feel different, no matter what you are actually feeling. Thus, even though you may have feelings of desperation, you can behave as if you don't.

This of course is not easy. As previously stated, if you are experiencing a barrage of venomous internal chatter, you are likely to exhibit behavioral signs that will communicate those feelings. Nevertheless, if you force yourself by *defining* yourself differently (although I feel anxious I am going to *play the role* of a confident person), you can experience a different behavioral outcome (you do not appear desperate) and may actually feel different.

Defining a Nonpressured Situation

There is also a trick you can play on your mind to make this even easier. That is, you can define the *situation* as less frightening.

What do I mean by this?

Let's say you were interviewed for a job that you had no interest in really acquiring. You just wanted to get the experience of an interview. If your classical way of interviewing is to appear hungry and accepting of whatever is offered, it would be quite easy to change that role in this situation. You could act like an "equal interviewer"—asking many questions about how the job would serve your needs, com-

fortably expressing your strengths, and even stating that certain criteria would have to be met in order for you to consider joining the team.

This could be accomplished rather easily because there is a dearth of
negative consequences. You don't really want the job. It doesn't matter
whether the interviewer likes you. You could flounder. You could sound
awkward. He or she could hate you. Who cares? *The goal is to practice
positive job interviewing skills, not to get this particular job.*

In the social arena you can easily create low anxiety situations by
defining an experience as an opportunity to learn instead of the night
you must meet Mr. Right. You can simply *decide* (yes, you have that
power*)* that you will not pursue finding someone during a particular
occasion. *You must not take phone numbers or connect with anyone
no matter who is there and no matter what happens.* This won't be
easy, but the benefits of this exercise far outweigh "losing" a night
now and then.

With the lack of a need to connect, you can behave in a confident,
relaxed manner. You can learn that you have the necessary social
skills or acquire them as you practice. You can sit back, observe the
social interaction, and observe how others appear desperate or appropriate. These models can teach you what to do or what not to do. You
can slow down and learn to listen to what others are communicating.
Exhibiting the ability and willingness to listen is a very strong social
skill that is very attractive to others. This exercise can also teach you
on a visceral level that there is no hourglass spilling sand, that a party
can begin and end without finding a boyfriend, and that the sky won't
come crashing down. This experience can further demonstrate that
you can't force relatedness—there has to be chemistry. If you do
enough "practicing," you can apply your knowledge to real situations
resulting in a very serious reduction of your own desperate patterns
behavior.

Now let's explore some other ways to decrease anxiety when
you're actually in a real social situation.

Anxiety Reduction Before You Go

Hours before you leave, start to work on relaxing. I do *not* recommend chemicals. You may want to take a hot bath, or do some physical
exercise, meditate, do deep breathing—whatever works for you. Leave
plenty of time to get ready so you are not rushing. Most important,

work on telling yourself that this is just going to be a nice event and although you'd like to meet someone, you don't absolutely *have* to.

Be Yourself

Turn your highly critical voice to "off." Just be yourself. Tell a joke if you want to. Be open about how you feel about something. Get comfortable with being you. You may be surprised about how OK this will be for many people.

Monitor Your Behavior

This may seem to be the opposite of what I just said, but it isn't. Keep the critic quiet but be aware of behavior that conveys desperation. This could be

- rapid speech
- not listening to what someone is saying while planning what you're going to say
- verbal domination—you don't let him get in a word
- looking at other guys when you're talking to one in particular
- concern about how much time you are spending with someone you don't feel particularly attracted to
- watching and being concerned about others who are making connections, particularly with those you find attractive

In a gentle manner, see if you can change some of this. Slow down your speech, stop looking at others, and stop looking at your watch. These changes may help you be calm and more like your true self.

About "Availability"

While you're relaxed in your search and clear about the characteristics of a real life partner, it's imperative that you focus your search on available men. What's the point of divesting energy on a great guy who's not available?

Availability is not determined solely on whether he's already involved. It also has a lot to do with where he is psychologically.

Screaming from rooftops that one wants a boyfriend doesn't mean availability. Availability means being ready for a relationship, and this is a complex issue. Realistically understanding and accepting what's involved and being motivated and willing to commit are but a few of the requisites.

Perhaps nothing is more demoralizing and a bigger waste of time than pursuing unavailable men. These relationships do not work out, yet much energy is expended on high drama, anger, disappointment, grieving, and outright misery. Internalized homophobia is fueled in these experiences—it becomes a challenge not to be convinced that all gay men are a "waste," and difficult to get back in the saddle. Therefore, avoiding unavailable men should be a priority.

Chapter 5 discusses how to do this and also explores how to determine the availability of someone familiar to you—*yourself.*

Chapter 5

How to Meet an Available Man

Tommy is a forty-one-year-old physician living in Seattle, Washington. He has been with his partner Phillip for nine months. At first their relationship seemed to be working. Both expressed being in love with one another, and they appeared happy. Recently Phillip lost his job as a manager in a dot-com company. He has been moody and irritable and questioning whether he still wants to work in the high-tech field. Of late he has not been emotionally available for Tommy. He is aware of this and has assured Tommy that this will pass. Tommy, nevertheless, is quite upset by Phillips's changed mood and doubts now whether he still wants to be with him. What he loved about Phillip was his "strength"—the way he could "take over" and give Tommy respite after being a responsible cardiologist all day. He misses that role and resents feeling he has to be there for Phillip.

Jefferson and Melvin live in Freeport, Long Island. Both twenty-four, they have been together for five months. The first few weeks were exuberant. Sex was heavenly and Jefferson loved talking with Melvin about their future plans. They would buy a house in the Napa Valley of Northern California, own a dog, and essentially live happily ever after. As the weeks turned to months, the sex calmed down and life became less magical for Jefferson. Melvin continues to express love and devotion to Jefferson, but this just makes Jefferson frustrated. His feelings for Melvin have grown cold. He feels like a fool for having had such "wild" thoughts only months ago. For the past two weeks he's been secretly dating another guy. He feels excited with his new boyfriend and is trying to figure out a way to let Melvin down easily.

Julio, a forty-seven-year-old businessman in Madison, Wisconsin, was very excited about Robert, a fifty-two-year-old social service administrator he met while in line at the bank. Within three weeks, Julio realized that Robert had a serious problem with drugs and alcohol. Robert was usually high when they got together, and he openly admitted that he was mixing Xanax and beer. He even bragged about coming to work loaded and no one having the slightest idea. Friends warned Julio that he once again was getting involved with a problem. Julio could not disagree more. In fact, Robert's problem was a sort of turn-on for him. He knew that Robert was needy, which made him feel needed. He even experienced vicarious thrills in the way Robert lived on the edge. The many men he met who seemed to live "constructive" lives bored him—they reminded Julio of himself.

However, Julio was devastated one evening when he arrived at Robert's apartment for a dinner date and found another man there. Robert was very drunk. Both men were in different states of undress and it was obvious they had been having sex. Robert asked Julio to join them in a threesome. When he refused, Robert called him a "pathetic asshole." Both Robert and the strange man laughed at Julio and then Robert ordered Julio to "get the fuck out of my house and out of my life."

Not unlike the majority of worthwhile objectives in life, flourishing relationships cannot be achieved without serious work. That effort begins long before the first date.

In these vignettes, at least one of the men in each couple was ill prepared for a serious commitment. Tommy did not understand that a relationship meant he also had to be there for his partner. Jefferson didn't appreciate that a relationship is more than enchanted moments. Julio's internal demons made him attracted to people that were unquestionably vacant.

The work or readiness that relationships need does not mean toil, but it does mean being realistic, adult, responsible, motivated, clear, psychologically healthy, and much more—a tall list certainly. However, there is good news. Some people out there fit the bill. If you don't fit the bill yet, you can still get there.

As we explore the signs and signals that evidence availability or the lack thereof, you need to look first and foremost at yourself. Although this chapter is written primarily from the perspective of assessing others (which is also extremely important), it's imperative that you first do the same evaluation on yourself. If you're not ready, the most available man on the planet won't be right for you.

Motivation

You first have to ask yourself if you truly want a relationship at this time in your life. This may seem simple, but it's not. Sometimes we are so influenced by peer pressure and cultural stereotypes that it's hard to see what we truly desire. This happens with career choices. I have met doctors and lawyers and psychotherapists who were not happy being doctors and lawyers and psychotherapists. Family pressure, societal pressure—the promise of money, power, control, or whatever—conspired to make these people think they wanted something they clearly did not.

One of the ways you can determine if you want a relationship is to be clear whether you feel you are going *to* or *from* something. If you feel essentially good inside your skin and your life, and believe a lover can enhance that already whole existence, you are probably on the right track. If you are depressed, scared, lonely, frustrated, empty, etc., and want a man to take away these problems, you are looking for inner peace (a very positive goal) but not a relationship. A relationship won't meet those needs. Inner peace comes from *within*. Take care of those issues (via therapy, etc.) and then reassess your motivation for a partnership.

When you meet a man you find interesting, listen to what he says about his desire for a relationship. Although I rarely advise taking anything at face value, someone who tells you he doesn't want a relationship right from the get-go shouldn't be second guessed. Some men see this as "the great challenge"—the majestic opportunity to convince a lost soul that he really does want a lover.

"He just hasn't found the right guy yet," you say.

Who will be that "right guy"?

"I will," you answer.

I don't think so.

Whatever his issues are, any man who says he's not looking is at the very least significantly ambivalent. You don't need that. Relationships are complex enough. You don't need to become involved with someone who is not even sure he wants to be there in the first place. He just might be telling you the unadulterated truth: *he* doesn't want it.

Lower your blood pressure. Move on.

Maturity and Knowing What It's About

First the good news: You don't have to meet some mythical standards of adulthood and self-actualization to create a successful relationship. But you can't be in Kid Land with unrealistic notions of what it's all about.

An understanding of the animal—that there will be ups and downs, that honesty and intimacy are cardinal, that people change and you have to work at accommodating change, all this and much, much more—is paramount for you to be available for such a major life experience.

One of the best ways to learn about relationships is by being in one. This implies that someone who has never been in a serious relationship would have more difficulty, which is likely to be true. Very often, and understandably, a first experience is not the last but rather a good learning experience.

For someone interested in a guy who may not have been around the block much or at all, please don't tell him you have to end the budding romance because Neil Kaminsky said he's just going though a learning experience at your expense! A first serious relationship can be long term and work out well. The novice does have to come with substantial realistic expectations and an open mind to learning. The more experienced man has to be tolerant of his partner's need to flounder and discover perhaps more than an experienced man would.

There is also no guarantee that a man who has been in multiple relationships is knowledgeable and realistic. His long track record may even be an indication that he's not. Some men refuse to give up science fiction. They hide behind walls of denial and cling to ideas of love as perpetual infatuation, hot-buffed young bodies, lack of conflict, and a host of other fantasies. Although this formula repeatedly fails them, they don't learn. These are men to avoid.

When you are in the early process of assessing, ask him about his vision. This doesn't mean you are cornering him into having a relationship with you; you just want to know about his ideas. This is a fair subject when you are getting to know someone. If he has ex-lovers and talks about them, find out what went wrong. You can learn a lot of information about his beliefs and expectations.

Of course, we have to get back to *you* now. What do you know about relationships? What do you expect? What have been your experiences?

One way to discover blind spots is to look at your personal history. If you've had some problematic relationships, ask yourself what went wrong with them. Work hard as hell to get away from blaming your ex and instead look at your role in the difficulties. Were you expecting too much fun or even too much work? As the relationship changed (less sex, for example) were you able to accept this or did you panic and think something was terribly wrong? How did you deal with those little annoying habits of his that drove you crazy? Did it seem strange that someone whom you loved could also annoy you, or did you see that as part of the relationship? How did you communicate (or not)? Did you become Sitting Bull when you were angry or did you tell him what was wrong? Did you tell him in an effort to problem solve or with the aim of blaming and shaming?

In the more affirmative, what did you do that really worked? What lessons (before today) did you learn after you parted that said, "That's why this didn't work, and I now know differently for the next time around"?

Knowing what a relationship is about prepares you for love. You will more easily identify men who are equally knowledgeable.

Searching for the Unavailable

Julio, in the previous vignette, is a perfect example of someone seeking unavailable partners.

Early on, Robert clearly demonstrated significant barriers to being accessible. He was not only out of control with booze and drugs, but engaged in reckless behavior. Going to work loaded and bragging about it speaks volumes. Given all of this, how could Julio expect him to be mature and responsible as a partner?

The fact is, he really didn't.

The biggest clue to this is in Julio's history. At times, for whatever reason(s), we can become dazzled with someone who is clearly inappropriate. Julio's friends, however, were concerned that he was getting involved with Mr. Wrong *again.* Indeed, this was a pattern for Julio.

The causes for this problem are complex. Often a material factor is substantial low self-esteem. You feel lousy about who you are so you create an outside world which reflects that.

Sometimes this plays out in an effort to "rescue" someone. You "accept" someone no one wants and he will "need" you. "Someone no one wants" is less threatening—someone everyone wants, you believe, would never want you. His "need" for you means you are important—it's an attempt to bolster your very fragile sense of self-worth.

This is likely an unconscious process. Needless to say, it doesn't work. The dramatic, miserable ending for Julio is fairly typical.

On the Rebound

Different penis, same man.

Brian Wolfe, MFT
Private Practice, San Francisco, California

You cannot be available for a new relationship if you are still involved with a previous one. You can be very involved in the old relationship even if you are no longer "involved."

Men who are on the rebound are among the most unavailable men on the planet. Rebounding is a complicated, destructive process. The essential problem is that a person gets involved with another in *reaction* to loss. He is using the new relationship (often unconsciously) as a way to deal with his loss. This is even true for men who were in very bad relationships and are truly happy to be uncoupled. There is still loss to grieve that will compromise any new relationship. The very likely outcome is that the new relationship will be short-lived and the end won't be pretty.

When I speak to groups of gay men, I am often asked how much time should pass. I can't give a definitive number—if I could, I would also be able pick winning lottery numbers! I will say this, though: if a relationship has been significant, the downtime must be significant as well. A person coming out of a relationship needs time not only to grieve but time to be alone, to recoup, and to reassess. If he doesn't do that, he *can't* be ready for you, as much as he may want to be.

If you meet a great guy who is going through a loss, give him time. I understand this will not be easy. You may not see him again. On the other hand, he may come back when he's ready. Sometimes the best way to reach someone is by letting go.

If you are the one who recently uncoupled, it's equally important for you to take a break. Many gay men I have worked with or interviewed find this difficult. Although they often accept it in theory, denial oozes through. They are dating a week after the breakup, or even before the breakup, and tell me it's not rebounding. They say they are just dating.

They are rebounding.

The big lie about rebounding is that it will ease your pain. You're not used to being alone and need to have a man by your side. But a relationship is much more than fulfillment. It means having the emotional energy for another person. When you still have to grieve and let go of a former lover, you don't have that emotional energy.

Ability to Give

Much of a relationship *is* about "getting." Even when you are there for your partner, there is often personal gratification—you soothe him and you feel good about making him feel good. But a relationship also means giving.

Sometimes you will have to be there for him when you don't want to. On occasion there's no payoff; you just have to give. You may have to visit the relatives, or deal with his nagging, or live through his conflicts at work.

Sometimes you have to give all you have. Taking care of a dying lover is such a time.

For those who have been a caretaker to a dying lover or friend, you know what that role is all about. It's about slowly losing someone you love in the most painful and cruel of ways. It's about dementia and pain and diapers. It's not a pretty sight, and no matter how much you love someone, caregiving takes a massive toll.

I am not referring only to the HIV pandemic. Life is lethal. If you are with someone long enough, you may experience tragedy.

Certainly, this is the extreme and not something you want to contemplate when you enter a relationship, but I believe you should consider it. It's a good litmus test of how much you are able to give.

The ability to give—and to give in a healthy manner (not in a codependent manipulative way)—is greatly determined by how internally satisfied you feel. This is not about money or status but about being happy and peaceful and fulfilled from *within*. No, you don't have to be the most actualized man on the planet, but if you are having significant struggles and problems in your life, honestly ask yourself whether you can meet the needs of a relationship. Analogous to rebounding, if your emotional energy is somewhere else, you won't have it to give to a lover.

This doesn't mean never, but does it mean taking care of yourself and learning ways to self-nurture. You must get your house in order to be available for a partner.

It's important to assess a potential partner's ability to give. Early on, you will not know him well, and it would certainly be precipitous to ask whether he would care for you if you became ill. You can also learn much about his capability by looking at his life.

Busy Guys

Busy, successful guys are very attractive. They have a life and we don't have to give them one. But you should ask—just how busy is he?

We often don't realize that a relationship is a serious time commitment. You can't squeeze a relationship in between a seventy-hour job, night classes, and monthly travel. It's a prescription for chronic frustration. If your potential boyfriend is married to his job, he won't be able to marry you.

He Has a Lover or All He Talks About Is His Ex(es)

This is a short section because we have essentially covered it. If he is still "technically" involved with a lover (he's about to break up, they have been talking about it, they have gone back and forth many times), wish him a good day and move on.

If his mental vista is filled with images of his ex(es), even if he broke up a long time ago, he can't be there for you. Some men forego grieving at the appropriate time (rebounding is one reason this happens) and are chronically and pathologically attached to an ex. The ex could even be dead.

If you recognize this, you have a simple task. Say good-bye.

Serious Emotional Problems

A person who has considerable difficulties with daily functioning is not someone who is available. Those problems need to be taken care of first.

Untreated depression, other forms of mental illness, chemical and alcohol dependency, sexual addiction, and other behavioral addictions such as gambling, etc., preclude the ability to fully participate in a relationship. This doesn't mean that such men can't be excellent partners when their lives are back in control. Sometimes having the experience of very deep pain and transcending that pain makes one very sensitive and very attractive indeed.

However, these kinds of problems *cannot* go away without professional intervention. Anyone who tells you he will stop using drugs on his own or stop having compulsive sex, for example, is giving you fair warning to run. Denial is a cardinal characteristic of addictions, and such a person is in denial. Without cracking that denial, there is *no* hope for change.

I'm not asking you to be a mental health professional, but if you have suspicions don't ignore them. Someone who is often high, who is sad and irritable a great deal, or who frequents sex clubs habitually may have serious problems. These are, of course, only a fraction of the possible signs you could see.

Ask him what is going on and see how he responds. You may also want to consult with a person trained to evaluate these conditions. There are many counselors who deal with chemical and other addictions, and you may be able to get some professional feedback by phone. In the final analysis, if you're not sure, use your best judgment. If you don't trust your judgment, talk to a friend or co-worker—someone who you feel is reasonably objective.

I'll be blunt about this. You will save yourself a lot of heartache if you avoid connecting with someone whose life is out of control.

Value and Interests

Opposites rarely attract. You might be amazed at his ability to take a year off from work and bike through Pakistan. You may wish you could do that, but if that's not where you're coming from, what at first seems fascinating will grow old. Fast.

What he likes, his job, his views of the world, his fundamental values about honesty, integrity, loyalty, etc., are all important. Sometimes a pretty face and a hot body have a way of obscuring these issues. The intensity of sexuality, as awesome as it may seem, does not a relationship make. If this man does not share many of your basic outlooks, frustration and disappointment will reign. You still have to keep your brain working as you experience sexual bliss. Of course, there is nothing wrong about having a hot sexual affair if you realize from the beginning that your affair is all that it is.

Pursuing men with similar views implies that you know yourself. Those of you with more insight will find this easier, but if you are somewhat unclear, you can do some work to find out.

Take a look at your life. Try to differentiate societal expectations from what is *significant to you*. What do you like? What kind of people fulfill you? Why? What kind of activities satisfy you? What kind of work do you do? What part of it is gratifying (e.g., if you like dealing with people you may be very "social")? What part of it can't you stand? What are your goals? Where do you want to be five years from now, ten years, etc.?

Getting in touch with your own values and desires will help you find someone who is compatible. Incompatible means unavailable.

Angry, Bitter, and Jaded

These men are out there, and they are not few. Some people are so battered by life that they can see only the darkness.

Some gay men walk around in a rage. They have been hurt, and they are angry with all those who have made life so miserable for them. They see gay life, and perhaps all of existence, as devoid of opportunities, devoid of change, devoid of hope. They are legendary victims in their own minds. They act the part of "looking for a relationship" but they long ago gave up on believing that any good ones exist.

Then along comes nice you and the message you get is "prove to me you're different." Not wanting to turn down a challenge, and knowing that you really are different, you set out to change this guy. He will see how different you are, his nastiness will melt, and you will both live happily ever after.

I'd say you have a better chance of going to Mars for a weekend getaway than having a relationship with a guy like this!

Some gay men do have good reasons to be bitter. Some are really nice fellows who are hurting desperately. They use rage and hopelessness as a defense against further assault. Some change with help. Some remain embittered to their graves.

All of which is beside the point.

Such men are simply not available for a relationship. Whatever you do, eventually you will be seen as persecutory. Without help, these men can't see anything but victimization. Cardinal psychodynamics include skewed perception, feelings of powerlessness, and an abdication of responsibility in creating one's own misery.

At the outset, bitter men will not necessarily appear as the frightening creatures just described. However, their rage is not usually far from the surface. Accusations early in your association, numerous tales of people hurting him with no account of his role, significant irritability, moodiness, and sarcasm are all bad signs.

You can't win with such fellows. You're looking for a relationship, not a nightmarish struggle in which the outcome has already been decided.

Liars

Trust and honesty are the cornerstones of intimacy. Furthermore, telling the truth is serious pro-relationship behavior. It means *dealing* with a situation instead of avoiding it. Dealing gives everyone the opportunity to problem solve, including the option to decide that the problem(s) cannot be solved and the relationship is not viable. Terminating a truly nonviable relationship *is* solving a problem.

Although none of us can claim sainthood, telling falsehoods, particularly in the early days of courting, is worrisome.

If someone you just met tells untruths, it is reasonable to assume that he is not very honest. You could be wrong, but without any other knowledge why should you think differently? Furthermore, first impressions are very significant. With the climate of distrust so many gay men live in, it may be very difficult for you to trust him in the future.

Lying is relationship poison. If you encounter it, assume you have just met an unavailable man.

The Closet

Coming out is a developmental issue. Someone who has come out long ago versus someone who is first exploring or still in the closet exist in very different worlds.

It's easy to get caught up in the politics of the "rightness" of being out, in the community ramifications, in the question of "outing" powerful people, and so on. But this doesn't mean anything if, for example, you came out twenty years ago and a guy you meet is still lying to his mother. Psychologically, he can't be where you are tomorrow or next year even if he desired that.

Different places on the closet spectrum mean significant challenges. You want to hold hands in public; he finds that intolerable. You want to meet his family; he knows he will be disowned. You feel that hiding is the apex of self-contempt; he believes that coming out is life threatening.

Challenges certainly can be met, and people do change. Someone not as out as you or vice versa is not categorically unavailable. On the other hand, you must be clear about what you're getting yourself into. These challenges are real. Be sure you can live with them.

Be frank in the beginning about where you are and ask him where he is. If he is truthful, it won't be difficult to figure out how close or far apart you are. Who is he out to? How does he handle public displays of affection? What are his beliefs about being gay? His goals about living as an openly gay man? His internalized homophobic feelings? Where are you at in these areas? What can you handle? What will not be acceptable?

Finding your clone is not your goal. You can be in different psychological places and learn from one another. You can reevaluate long-held positions and grow. Conversely, if you are on diametrically opposite poles, neither of you is probably available for the other.

Significant Age Variance

As with the closet, considerable age differences do not, in and of themselves, preclude the possibility of a successful relationship. Indeed, as mentioned earlier in the book, when we refuse to consider someone because of his age, we may be forgoing opportunities.

On the other hand, a twenty-three-year-old and a sixty-five-year-old have very different life experiences. Can that chasm be gratifying as well as challenging? Is there a monetary and/or power dynamic that will adversely affect them? Is the young man really seeking money? Is the older man seeking control and vicarious eternal youth?

Even without these potential problems, there is a hard fact to contend with in terms of longevity. A sixty-five-year-old man is likely to die long before his twenty-three-year-old partner. Is this something the younger partner, or for that matter the older one, accepts, understands, and can live with?

The difference in age used in the previous example is an extreme. A smaller age difference will still be significant—how significant certainly depends on the age difference, but it also has a lot to do with the individuals. If you meet someone appreciably older or younger than yourself, your best guide is to be clear about what you want, why you want it, and the challenges before you. Being realistic can create the foundation for an enduring, healthy bond. It can also save you the heartache of pursuing something that isn't right for you.

Denying the influence of dissimilar "life space" can backfire. Seeking control, money, power, eternal youth, and so on are good reasons not to pursue such a union.

Long-Distance Love Affairs

Daniel met Logan during a vacation in Provincetown, Massachusetts, in the summer of 2000. Logan lives in Boston, Daniel in Los Angeles. They had a wild, wonderful week in paradise. The sex was truly heavenly, incessant, and everywhere. They made love in the middle of the night, at four in the afternoon, on the beach, in the dunes, on the bike trails, and sometimes even in their rooms! They made each other laugh; they ate delicious shrimp and lobster; they drank gallons of chardonnay; and they held hands as they walked along the moonlit ocean shore.

Daniel is a thirty-five-year-old social worker who works with foster children in LA. He had hated his job for years and was looking to leave but was unsure of where to go. He had also been looking for love, he felt, for all of his life. After a week with Logan, he thought he found it.

Logan is a twenty-nine-year-old real estate broker in Boston. He had a few short-term relationships before he met Daniel. He had a wonderful time with him in P-town and thought he was in love also.

They had a long-distance relationship for six months. Telephone calls and on-line, they continued to profess their love for each other. Both talked about Daniel moving to Boston and staying with Logan until he found a job. In January 2001, Daniel made the decision to move, and on February 10, he moved in with Logan.

On April 22, Daniel was on a United Airlines flight back to Los Angeles. He was depressed and angry, primarily with himself. He castigated himself repeatedly for being so "stupid," and questioned how on earth he ever believed he was in love with Logan. He was even more flabbergasted at himself for leaving LA.

Everything changed, beginning the first day he moved in. Daniel missed his friends in LA and felt sad. He assumed Logan would be sensitive and supportive, but that was not the case.

"Well, now you're here, baby, so just get over that," Logan told him.

Within two days there were telephone calls from guys that Daniel never knew existed. He asked Logan about them.

"Well, you don't think I was celibate all those months when you were in LA? Of course I went out—but they are only friends now," Logan told Daniel.

"Well, I was celibate, and I don't know how comfortable I am with them being your 'friends'," Daniel replied.

And so it went, only much worse. Daniel found difficulty getting work and felt uncomfortable living in Logan's house. He became worried about money and felt no emotional support from Logan. The sex became less enjoyable, less frequent, and finally stopped altogether.

On April 1, Logan announced, "I think we should see other people."

That evening Daniel began planning his return to Los Angeles.

Meeting Someone on Vacation

Having a romantic fling when you are away from the pressures of life is like living, temporarily, a magnificent dream. To confuse that with appraising the potential for a long-term relationship can be a big mistake.

Daniel and Logan had very little real knowledge of each other. Their experience was only a week long with intense sex, lots of drinking, and an absence of daily living pressures. Furthermore, neither was seeing the other in his normal setting. That in and of itself precludes accurate assessing.

It's not that you can't start a viable relationship on a vacation. It simply means that you have to get to know the individual over a period of time when both of you are not on holiday. Phone calls and communication online are poor substitutes for one-on-one physical interaction.

Moving to Join Someone

I would think long and hard before moving to be with someone. No matter how much you may truly love him, moving will be a major change with very significant pressures. Getting used to a new city, making new friends, finding work, etc., will put a strain on you. Since a new relationship already is a major stress (no matter how equally wonderful), putting the two together is asking for trouble. In the case of Daniel, who didn't really know Logan, it was almost a guarantee for disaster.

Once again, it doesn't mean that moving across the country (or whatever distance) is always a mistake. But it shouldn't be done before a solid relationship is established. This means, foremost, giving it the proper time. It also means having numerous visits (more than just weekends) where you are getting a real idea of the new place and your new boyfriend.

Can Long-Distance Relationships Work?

Perhaps you meet someone who lives in a distant city and neither of you intend to move. Could you consider yourself and this man available for a relationship with each other?

You can't categorically dismiss this as impossible, but you must consider a number of factors.

Distance is sometimes a way to keep excitement going *because* there is no real relationship. The fantasy, the longing, and the romance stay alive because there's no day-to-day reality. In a sense, men in these unions don't really want a relationship—they want fantasy. Although this can be fun, it's very limited. Growing together as a couple, developing deeper feelings, and meeting and transcending challenges does not happen.

On the other hand, some long-distance relationships are "real." Although living physically apart, the men still cultivate a relationship. Part of this has to do with the men making the effort to see each other. Men in these relationships face the normative challenges of love and much more. A relationship conducted solely by e-mail and phone cannot mature.

Certainly the question of monogamy versus open agreement arises in such an arrangement. If monogamy is chosen, a high level of trust must be established.

Besides the issue of sexuality, there is the threat of "finding someone else." A long-distance relationship means lots of time apart. What happens if you meet someone who is "good husband material" and lives only a mile from you? You would have to forego that temptation and so would your partner. It's not only a question of trust. It's a question of accepting this fact of your relationship. Being physically apart can be lonely and depressing.

There are also the practical hassles. Long-distance relationships are expensive. The long-distance telephone calls and plane flights add up. There is also the effort of traveling or having a guest stay at your place on a regular basis. These may seem like minor problems until you start living with them.

Relationships involve lots of negotiations that often need to be done in person. If your partner lives a 1,000 away, you'll not always be able to do that when you should. For example, if a serious problem arises (e.g., one of you had sex with another man and the agreement is monogamy), it's best to address it as quickly as possible. The most serious of problems are often threatening to men, and we'd just as soon avoid such matters as long as possible. Sometimes putting off dealing with it turns into never dealing with it. Never dealing is relationship venom. If you and you lover can't get together for a month, that time period may serve to strengthen the tendency not to deal with problems. The emotional fire may have passed, and you both conspire to evade because "it's over." Of course it's not, and it's likely to come back and create serious obstacles.

We've touched upon what constitutes a real relationship, but in Chapter 6 we'll go further. We'll explore the nuts and bolts of being with a lover, what daily life is all about, what's reasonable to expect, and what amounts to castles in the sky.

Fantasies about love are rampant in American culture. This causes difficulties for many gay men because it creates expectations that cannot be met. Being successful in finding a life partner means having a clear vision of what real love and relationships are all about.

Chapter 6

Do You Really Want a Boyfriend?

We're relating to a kind of fantasy. The dream of finding a lover for many of the people I see . . . is that I will find this porn star God. . . . If you want to have a long-term relationship with anybody you ultimately have to wake up on a rainy Tuesday morning in bed with somebody who has bad breath and is putting on a little weight and is grouchy. . . . The reality of it is very different. Real relationships are not porn movies and they're not parties.

Thomas Moon, MFT
Private Practice, San Francisco, California

Finding a partner requires understanding what you are pursuing and why. Why do you want a partner? Why do you want him now? How will life be different when he's there? What will you get out of it? What are you searching for? What won't you like? How do you believe you will experience daily life?

You may deem these rather silly questions with obvious answers. However, they are important to consider, so get out a piece of paper and write down the answers.

Why? Because it will give you important information and you will get a good idea of your expectations. As we explore the process, you can learn which of your visions are real, which aren't, what you have to change, and what you won't and/or can't. It's even conceivable to discover that you don't want a relationship given what is *really* involved. Although this is probably not the case for the vast majority reading this book, if a relationship is not for you, it's better to learn this before you're in the middle of one.

It's also imperative to understand that many of the glitches you will inevitably encounter are normal. They are common, resolvable, and part of the terrain. The music does stop at times, but your relationship need not.

Starting with the Positive

This all being said, let's start by taking a look at what's so perfectly wonderful about being with the man of your dreams.

Hollywood conceptualizations of love would not exist if there were nothing to them. Being with a life partner can be one of the most fulfilling experiences you will ever have.

Falling in love and having a successful relationship colors life in a manner that's challenging to describe in words. You have someone to come home to, someone to share your triumphs and defeats, someone to grow with. He understands you as no other does, and there's profound safety and delight in knowing that he's there. Although your existence is meaningless to the vast majority of the human race, to your lover you mean everything.

A life partner is a supreme form of ego gratification. Out of everyone, he has chosen you. He's *in love with you*. Real love can't be bought, manipulated, nor contrived. It means the *real you* is so awesomely appealing to this man that it has caused an involuntary process within his soul—*he has fallen in love with you*.

Despite such a heavenly experience, both of you still reside in a place called Planet Earth. Life overflows with challenges that a relationship cannot avoid. In fact, your union will present you with trials and tribulations itself.

Day-to-Day Life

When the routine of life drives us crazy, we sometimes imagine that all will be different with a partner. I would think again. If you don't like laundry or cleaning or going to the supermarket, it's not apt to be much different with a partner. True, there may be less work if you are sharing responsibilities, but that still doesn't transform into fun. Hollywood images of preparing a meal together with romantic music, loving smiles, and radiant candles will not be your experience if you hate cooking. More likely, your partner will be asking why the hell you are watching TV while he's doing all of the work.

Responsibilities can also *increase* with a relationship even if you don't live together. Perhaps you have lived like a slob all of your life and not only hasn't it bothered you, you haven't noticed! Then along comes your man who refuses to eat off your dishes because it looks like Jimmy Hoffa may be hiding in your kitchen. Sure, it's still your house and you can do what you want, but more likely you'll need to compromise, which means doing something you ordinarily wouldn't do.

Daily life also involves some degree of boredom. When we are single we may think that this is so because we're unattached. We may pass a smiling couple as we head home with a gallon of Ben & Jerry's and muse about all the fun we're missing. But the image of the smiling couple as a constant is more fluff than substance. Of course, there will be fun times, perhaps ecstatic times, with your lover. There should be. But there will also be days when you are both tired and stressed and irritable and blame each other for having no ideas about what to do. You may long for the days you could veg out with Ben & Jerry's and have no one to aggravate you!

Time, Energy, and Even Money!

A relationship requires a significant investment of time and energy. Those under the misconception that a relationship is all about "getting" are usually surprised when they realize this investment is required. Indeed, many relationships don't make it because this was never accounted for.

Time and energy must not only be expended on "quality time" with your man. Even when you're not physically together you are responsible to him. If you have to work late every night and/or go on business trips, you have to take into account how this will affect him and the relationship. If he is not happy about this, you have to negotiate and find a middle ground. That could be very difficult if you have a demanding job and are trying to climb the ladder.

We also tend to spend more money when we're involved. Although expenses do go down if you move in together, it's the opposite when you're first courting.

This may seem a silly point, but it isn't if you are struggling with a budget. There are occasions to celebrate, the increased frequency you go out, the nice shirt you just had to buy him, the weekend trips, the many times he bought you breakfast so now it's your turn to pay for dinner, etc. Certainly this can be loads of fun, but it does add up and you should consider that as you think about finding a man.

The Ebb and Flow of Love

No feelings are static. If you look at a typical day in your life, you will experience a gamut of feelings. Love works in the same way.

There is no chance you will experience a constant sense of adoration for your beloved, nor him for you. Sometimes, loving feelings for no apparent reason will be less powerful than at other times. *And there may be no reason other than feelings naturally ebb and flow.* Sometimes you and your partner will be sick of each other and wish the other were not around. I don't mean dead or not in your life—just not around. Maybe for an hour. Maybe for a weekend.

When we are enraptured with Hollywood romance (and Hollywood has a way of penetrating the unconscious), you may think something is wrong when you're not so thrilled with him or he with you. You may put pressure on yourself or on him. "Is there something wrong, Johnny? Do you still love me?" Or you may wonder, "Am I falling out of love? This is not the way it's supposed to be."

Of course, this is a fail-safe way to *create* a real problem!

Love *is* about, as a friend of mine once said, making the mundane "all electric." But you can't expect that to be unremitting.

Bilateral Decisions

Major decisions in life are no longer just your own. Perhaps you wanted to move to another state, adopt a child, or spend a summer in Africa. Your new partner is now in your life and must be considered if you want him to remain in your life. This clearly means that you have less freedom when you are attached. It's true that the hallmark of a healthy relationship is growing individually and as a couple. You certainly need to maintain your individuation as you cultivate your joining together. This does not mean denying vital personal needs for the sake of the relationship. On the other hand, there is no getting around the fact that your man is part of your life's equation and that your freedom will be compromised to some degree. It's imperative to embrace this idea before you get involved.

The High-Wire Act of Merging and Separation

A relationship, in a sense, is a form of insanity. You must get powerfully close and maintain clear boundaries at the same time. If you don't let down the walls, you miss out on intimacy. If you and he "become one," you will both suffocate and someone will probably flee.

This is one of the most difficult jobs that all couples face. How do you profoundly care about him but not *become* him? How can his decisions change your life yet remain his decisions? How do you love him with all your heart but remember to love yourself first?

Although this task may get easier in time, it's always present and it takes a considerable effort to achieve balance.

You Are Exposed

Those who get close to us see the parts of us that we may not know and would rather not meet.

We all have our shadowy sides. Although you may be a great human being, you can also be, *at times,* petty and nasty and insensitive and jealous and revengeful and immature and dirty and racist and uncaring and stupid and—I can go on and on! Lovers see these sides of us—there is no way to hide them—and they are often eager to share their insights with us. I don't mean this as a way to humiliate or punish, although that does go on in destructive relationships. In the normal course of sharing a life together these parts become evident, and partners will let us know what they see.

It's no fun to hear from someone you love that you can be a real prick at times, especially when, upon reflection, you realize it's true. Thus a relationship is a powerful form of self-exposure.

Trust and Emotional Vulnerability

Trust, one of the cornerstones of intimacy, is risky and frightening. When you trust you let down barriers. You are vulnerable. You have high expectations. You can be hurt and disappointed. You are not in control.

Although this kind of emotional risk taking is not easy for anyone, gay men have special problems. As discussed, a cardinal imperative of homophobia is that gay men are not trustworthy. You have not only been told this; most of you have had some experiences in which you have in fact been let down by a gay man. That doesn't prove the supposition, but it certainly can feel that way.

Men in our culture do not easily embrace vulnerability. Men are strong, in charge, in control. Of course, that's sexist nonsense, but a lifetime of chauvinist messages takes its toll.

The royal dilemma of all this is that if you don't trust and accept vulnerability, the intimacy you're seeking will not be forthcoming.

This risk and conflict is just too great for some. This is when many precipitously bail from otherwise viable relationships. The anxiety may not even be conscious, which makes the dynamic even more damaging.

It's very important to recognize that any relationship will cause this unease. It's normal. It's not, in and of itself, the beginning of the end. It exists because relationships are scary, and a gay relationship in a homophobic, sexist society is even more frightening. Recognizing and preparing for this in advance can go a long way in preventing you from running. It's also a good idea to take a frank look, before you get involved, at your internalized homophobia and your feelings about intimacy, emotional vulnerability, and lack of control. If you have significant difficulties with these issues, it may be helpful to seek counseling from a gay affirmative therapist.

Sex

Easy, quick, no-strings-attached sex is part of the culture of the gay community. Although sex without commitment is limited and at times hollow, there is no question that there are certain advantages. Meeting a hot stranger online or in a distant city for a one-time rendezvous can be thrilling and dreamlike, not to mention fabulously pleasurable. And it's easy. You don't know him and he doesn't know you. It doesn't matter how you perform because you may never see him again. You can just go through a wild night of relaxed, raw bliss (safely, I hope) and smile broadly as you drink your morning coffee.

Not so with your boyfriend. Sex with a partner is a sexual *relationship*. You will see him again and you do know each other. As with all relationships, there are highs and lows, changes, and good and bad times. The relationship you have outside of the bedroom will impact your sexuality, as your sexual relationship will affect the rest of your lives together. It's complicated and not as easy as anonymous sex.

There is nothing awful or irresolvable about this. Indeed, sex with a lover can be more satisfying because you are in love with this person. It can also be exciting and wonderful. Having a partner *doesn't* mean you should look forward to an unsatisfying sex life. The problem comes when your expectations are based on the relative ease of anonymous encounters, or the "everyone is always equally horny twenty-four hours a day" porn movie portrayal of life. Having a bad time, getting bored, or going through a period when you or he are less interested happens in relationships. This is to be expected and they are not indications of impending doom. Understanding this before you get involved can go a long way in preventing a normal occurrence from becoming a crisis. It's also important that you buy into this—that you *accept* that this is what you get when you have a partner.

Accepting the Whole Package

Hopefully, both as individuals and as a couple you will change and grow in time. Remaining static is not a healthy way to negotiate the world.

On the other hand, you and your future partner are full-grown adults. To expect him to undergo a personality transformation or for you to be pressured by him to be someone you are not can be very damaging—not to mention futile.

Many gay men fall in to this trap once they are involved for a few months. You both discover parts of each other that you don't admire and you set out, consciously or unconsciously, to change the other person.

Constructive criticism is fine. If you or your partner *desires* to change what has been criticized, by all means make the effort. However, a world of difference exists between that and expectations and demands to be a different person in order to satisfy the other. That doesn't foster change; it creates resentment.

Doing a thorough assessment of the person in the very early days will produce less surprises. Often what shocks us later on was really there in the beginning. We failed to look or just didn't want to see.

It's also important to be yourself so you don't present a false impression. Nevertheless, we are all on our best behavior in the beginning. Some of what you don't like and some of what he'll find annoying will become evident only after you have been together for a while.

Once again, this is normal and to be expected. This is not to say you can't discover traits that are unacceptable. In that case, you really do have to question whether you want to remain involved. But if you expect the music to continue unabated, or you require Mr. Right to be Mr. Perfect, you're looking for a fantasy, not a real life partner.

So far, we have explored what is involved in a real relationship. We covered in an earlier chapter what a real life partner is—that is, the characteristics that enable participation in a committed adult relationship. We touched on your personal requirements of a partner—and which of them are realistic and which aren't. We also looked at availability and determining how to meet a man who will be available for what you need.

You probably have, by now, a good idea of what a relationship is all about. So what can you do with all this newfound knowledge?

How about literally *designing,* in advance, your next relationship?

Think about it. Skyscrapers could not remain standing nor could rockets fly into outer space without a good design in advance. Why should it be different with a relationship?

True, relationships are about humans, and they are not as predictable as steel and brick. To have expectations as specific as if developing the structure of a rocket engine is not what I'm talking about.

I am talking about good planning and a clear vision, which means understanding *you and what you need and desire.* Remarkably, having an unambiguous picture of your next relationship can go a long way toward making that become your relationship! Because human nature and love is so mysterious and perplexing, we often believe we have to leave it to fate or chance. We dare not ask for what we really want because, on a deep level, we don't believe we can really have it. We fear being disappointed.

I am asking you to risk disappointment, which in fact will dramatically cut your chances of it occurring. Think about it. This is your life, and when they cart you away on a cold day in 2050 (or much sooner) you won't have any more opportunities. Now is the time to find the man and relationship of your dreams. Chapter 7 will help you do that.

Chapter 7

Finding Yourself First

Just what do you want? What do you need? These may seem to be easy questions, but, in fact, they are profoundly difficult. Major mistakes in life often occur because we really don't know these answers. We take a job because of money and then we dread each day. We move to a new city to get away from problems, but they follow us. We bond with the "man of our dreams" who turns out to be the nightmare of our lives.

Getting What You Shouldn't Ask For

An excellent proverb proclaims, "Be careful of what you wish for, because you just might get it." It underscores this confusion. It also calls attention to the fact that *attaining* is not the problem; attaining *what's right* is the problem.

In the endeavor to find a partner, gay men get caught up in the false belief of scarcity and the erroneous focus on "just finding someone." This divests their energy from where it should be—figuring out who they are, what they want and need, and whom they could love and share time with. It's relatively easy to have a boyfriend. It's quite another matter to find a real life partner.

Wants and Needs

Not only do we have trouble answering the questions of what we want and need, but we often interchange these words. They are not necessarily the same. You may want a drink because it's New Year's Eve, but if your liver is pickled from chronic alcoholism, you don't *need* that drink.

Needs and wants in relationships are not as apparent as this example because there is no "biological certainty." You need water to survive, but you don't need a BMW. Once again, that distinction is obvious. What you need and/or want in a relationship is not. It's a matter of an individual judgment call, but a terribly vital one.

Please be clear, however, that needs and wants in relationships will often be the same, and there will be no reason for concern. You may want to trust your lover and you also need to be able to trust him. You may want a partner who is intelligent and you need this so you can experience parity. You may want your man to have good self-awareness and you need that in order to be comfortable discussing your feelings with him.

Wants and needs sometimes don't have to be the same, and still may not necessarily be problematic. You may want a six-foot muscular man in his thirties, but you can feel sexually and emotionally fulfilled with a lean, shorter man in his forties. If you do find the six-foot guy, good for you!

The problem comes *when your desires are in conflict with what's obligatory for your ultimate well-being.*

In Chapter 2, I discussed what a real life partner is and asked you to brainstorm about what you need in a man. I also asked you to write it down. Take out that list now. If you didn't do it, go back to Chapter 2 and proceed. In fact, even if you did the exercise, it wouldn't hurt to go through the process again. You may come up with more information. Using this information as a backdrop, I am now going to ask you to go a little further.

Take a look at the list and determine if some of the *needs* you indicated are actually incompatible *wants*. One way to determine this is to think of previous relationships. Is there anything on that list that stands out as a prima facie reason why your relationship crashed? If it's not quickly evident, look again. Any of those "needs" that played a vital role in the demise of a previous relationship may be an incompatible "want." If you see something that has repeatedly been involved in relationship failures, it's even more suspect.

Often we have some awareness of this, and it usually takes the form of pursuing men you "know" are not good for you but whom you think you somehow "need." The denial is often expressed in the thought that "this time it will be different."

This can manifest in many ways. You may chase guys who are too young, or who aren't responsible, or who have life experiences and values that are dramatically different from your own. You do get something out of this—perhaps a firm young body, or the impulsiveness you fantasize about, or the vicarious experience of viewing a life you would otherwise not have access to. But at the end of the day, this will not give you a relationship.

If you recognize these traits in yourself, you have some vital data about "needs" *that are really what you definitely don't need.* Rather, you *want* something at a significant cost, most likely the possibility of a viable relationship. It's important to make a commitment to yourself to acknowledge that these are not needs and to no longer pursue such men. You also have to commit to relinquishing the short-term gratification you do get.

If you can't do that, there may be a self-destructive process operating. For some reason(s), likely unconscious, you are trying to derail yourself. You are, in effect, giving yourself "false treats" while making love and happiness elusive.

You may truly desire a viable relationship. This kind of a conflict, which is not uncommon, doesn't have to remain with you forever. You can find the right relationship. But you have some work to do to get to the bottom of why you are getting in your own way.

More About You

It's true that some of us understand ourselves relatively well and others go through life without insight. But here is some good news. Unless you were born yesterday, you have a life history with loads of data about the person you are. You just have to recognize that information.

I am going to ask you to do an exercise. The focus isn't on the man you're looking for but on what *you* are all about (which of course will help you seek the right man). One basic rule as you go through this: *no judging, no criticizing of yourself.* Unquestionably, that would place a wall between yourself and gaining insight.

For those who feel they know themselves well, I suggest you do the exercise anyway. There is always something you can discover about yourself, and the more you know, the better position you'll be in to find a partner.

The exercise I am going to present will be visualization along with series of questions. The questions may stimulate you to come up with questions of your own. That's great. Don't feel, however, that you have to come up with *answers* right away. The purpose is to get you thinking and feeling. You will also need to come back to this a number of times. This is a learning *process,* not a quiz.

It's imperative to give yourself proper emotional space for this exercise. That essentially means being in a place where you are calm, undistracted, not interacting with others, and not in any kind of a hurry. The last thing you need is to rush yourself through this because you have an appointment to keep.

For some, doing a relaxation exercise first will be necessary (Davis, McKay, and Robbins Eshelman, 1982). Others may discover that doing the exercise as soon as they wake up is best. Still others may find it's best before they go to sleep. You can experiment. Whatever makes you more open to introspection is what you should be doing.

Learning Your Core Values

What's most important to you in this life? It's probably a question you've asked before.

A good way to explore this question is to envision how it would feel to be dying.

I am going to ask you to visualize a very scary picture. Imagine yourself on your deathbed. You are dying of some kind of cancer. You are years younger than you ever imagined you'd be at the time of your death. You're weak, bedridden, and can't eat. Perhaps you're at home with loved ones by you. Maybe you're in a hospital. Maybe worse—a nursing home. As frightening as this may seem, try to experience the image as clearly as possible. Look at the walls, the ceiling, yourself in the hospital bed, the faces of people nearby. See the windows, the colors, the lack of colors, the sterile white sheets, the rails on the bed, the oxygen tube in your nose. Feel the heat or the cold. See the darkness outside the windows or the burning sun illuminating the room. Hear the noises. Perhaps people are talking about you or trying to talk to you and don't think you understand. Maybe they're crying. Study their sad faces. Smell the odors, perhaps alcohol and disinfectant. Feel your weakness, your pain, your lethargy, your loss of function, your loss of hope, your loss of options, your loss of a future.

Very little time is left. Although you are very weak and sleepy, your mind is clear. You now question: What really *mattered* in the life I'm about to exit? What made this journey worthy of its existence?

What did I really care about? What did I really want? What made me happy? What fulfilled me? What am I going to miss the most? What do I wish I had done? What should I have spent more time doing? What were the big mistakes? What did I do right? What am I proud of? What am I ashamed of? What seemed important that I now realize was meaningless? Who were the people that were significant? Why? Who did I really love? What is love? What deception passes for love? How important is love to me? Who am I going to miss the most? Who do I wish I had never met? What kind of a lover did I never meet that I wish I had? What would he have been like? How would he have fulfilled me? What do I now *know I'd do differently in my life if only I got another chance?*

You will need to explore these questions numerous times. This will take effort and time. It will take many of these "sessions." These are very complex questions with many answers.

Some of the subjects may not be applicable or you may not be able to find answers. Don't push yourself if you feel puzzled or can't answer. Just revisit the question at another time. If you never get to an answer, so be it.

Creating the *emotional feeling* about dying is paramount to opening up. The more detailed you can make the death scene in your mind's eye, the more real it will feel, and the more likely it will have emotional significance. That's what you want—an *unambiguous visceral reaction.*

This will give you a great deal of information about who you are. Obviously this is good not only for your pursuit of a partner, but also for your pursuit of happiness. The very good news as you come out of this terrifying scene is that *you do have another chance starting this very minute.* You can expend your energy on "what really mattered in the life I'm about to exit" and not on what "seemed important that I now realize is meaningless." Evidently, you are now armed with a blueprint for a relationship. If money and prestige in a partner is really meaningless but having kindness in his heart is vital, you will have no trouble figuring out whom you want to be with.

Your Relationships Up Until Now

On a lighter note, let's take a look at your relationships. I am not referring to lovers but to friends and other people you know. What kind of people are granted access into your life? What major characteristics exist in you friends? What makes you feel supported, stimulated, comfortable, and happy in their presence? These same characteristics need to exist in a partner.

Looking at it from the other perspective, what kind of people aren't allowed access? What don't you like about those people? What makes their presence uncomfortable?

Obviously, the traits of these people should not be shared by the people you are dating. Sometimes this happens because of the old "thinking with the wrong head" phenomenon. You know by now that those personality dynamics will surface with a vengeance as soon as your lower head stops saluting! These people should not be seriously considered, and it's best to exit a budding relationship with such a person before things become seriously unhappy.

Feedback from Good Friends

Despite all of our introspection tools, sometimes we are blind to information about ourselves that only others can see. If you have friends who are supportive, reasonably objective, and comfortable enough to honestly tell you how they see you (both the good and the bad), have some conversations with these people. You might ask them to tell you what kind of a relationship they think would work best for you. This doesn't mean you necessarily have to agree. It's just another way to get more information that may help you with any blind spots you have.

Putting It All Together

By this point you should have a fairly good idea about who you are and what you're looking for. Let's refine that information by addressing a few more points.

There is a lot more freedom today in both gay and heterosexual relationships to choose the life *you* want. Thus, when "designing" your future relationship, think big! Maybe you want to date a number of men simultaneously to give yourself a lot of choice. Go for it as long as you are honest with all of the men. Let's say you *don't* want to eventually "settle down" and live together—that's possible. Some gay partners have separate residences. Maybe you want to have, in

due course, outside sexual liaisons or threesomes with a partner—
why not, if both of you are comfortable with such an arrangement?
Maybe you want to adopt children, or have a baby with a surrogate, or
never have children. All of these choices are possible. We really can
choose, to a large degree, the lives we want. Think boldly, and then go
out and find someone who shares your perspective.

It can also help to think about your future relationship in significant detail. What will day-to-day life be all about? What role do you
want your and his families to play in your relationship? How out to do
you want to be? What part of the country or the world do you ultimately want to live in? What will you want to do with him on Sunday
afternoons, during the evenings, while on vacation? What kind of a
sexual relationship do you want? What will be the fun in your relationship and what will be the hassles? What will you be able to accept, and what will be unacceptable? What will you love sharing with
him? What will you still want to do on your own?

What do you expect him to give you, and are you able to give what
you expect? That is a key issue. We can't demand that which we cannot provide. If you want a supportive man, for example, you have to
be supportive. If you want honesty, you have to be honest. If you have
trouble with that, what could you do to change?

This being said, designing your relationship doesn't mean you'll
get *everything* you plan for. You must take into account "the human
factor" which always puts a glitch or two into the plans of men (and
women). Furthermore, we're all human. There is no perfect relationship. However, having all this information beforehand will put you in
an exceedingly advantageous position. Many of us get into relationship disasters because we don't have a clue what we're seeking until
we realize we're waist deep in what we definitely don't want.

Clarity about the kind of relationship you're seeking is not the only
sphere of knowledge you must exhibit. Your expectations and beliefs
about gay relationships are exceedingly important. A pessimistic
view, even subconsciously buried, can wreak havoc on the best of
plans. If you fundamentally believe that "gay relationships can never
work out," for example, you may actually *bring* that about without
even realizing it! This is the self-fulfilling prophecy, and it's lethal.

In Chapter 8 we will learn how internalized homophobia, previous
relationship trauma, and collective community opinion can screw up

your next relationship before you even begin it. The good news: knowledge is power, and you can prevent this disaster. You can develop positive expectations and create a psychological milieu in which you can find a relationship that will flourish.

Chapter 8

Expecting the Worst and Getting It

It is unrealistic to think your partner will be one hundred percent faithful. It is unrealistic to think a (gay) relationship will last forever.

> Billy, twenty-eight
> Student, Boston, Massachusetts

Gay relationships often do not last . . . gay men often meet at bars, clubs, bathhouses, and bushes.

> Henry, forty-seven
> Corporate Trainer, Chicago, Illinois

It is very hard to believe a man who says "I don't sleep with others." I don't think gay men are monks.

> Jackson, thirty-seven
> Software Developer, Palo Alto, California

We are very powerful creatures, but often aren't cognizant of our control. A great deal of what we perceive as "happening" to us is really *determined* by us. If you have a strong belief, you can create that which you believe. Without realizing it, you are designing your own reality. If your conviction is destructive, that's what you'll bring forth.

This is no less true with relationships. There are limitations to our influence, but they are terribly less significant than the limitations we place on ourselves. Abysmal gay men exist but it's *you* who permit such men access to your life. There are also wonderful men available, and you can find them. Yes, *you can find such men and one of those men can become your life partner!* However, if you have "determined" that most or all gay men are scoundrels, you won't be able to see a magnificent gentlemen. This process of predetermination will be at the perimeter of your awareness if not totally inaccessible. However, its damage will be palpable. When it's operating, the true Mr. Right can be in your face and you won't see him. He may visit your life for a while, but then *you* will do things to create circumstances that make him seem unsuitable. Your mind will subsequently proclaim "Ah ha! I knew it all along!" You'll break up, be more certain of your conviction, and never realize what happened.

Or you may seek out and find men who are truly bad news and generalize this to the entire gay male population.

Even worse, you could behave in a manner that "lives out" a damaging belief even though your behavior is not an accurate reflection of your heart. You may find yourself lying, cheating, and treating others as objects. You may remember a time when you were very different but justify your transformation on the grounds of being hurt too many times. To be any different, you reason, would be foolish. At the core of this is *the conviction that this is the way it is; that this is what it means to be a gay man.* Herein lies the self-fulfilling prophecy. A belief produces behavior that "confirms" the principle by manufacturing a "reality" (your behavior) that is evidence for both yourself and the man you're hurting that all gay men are pricks! When you multiply this reasoning times a few hundred thousand gay men, a rather ghastly "reality" is produced.

Self-Fulfilling Prophecy Defined

A self-fulfilling prophecy is a means by which a belief(s) creates behavior that brings about circumstances which appear to confirm the initial belief. The salient point is that the original belief creates the reality (or the apparent reality), not the other way around. This "reality" is then seen as "evidence" for the original belief. It's actually evidence only of a self-fulfilling prophecy. Because you're unlikely to be aware of this process operating, it's difficult to appreciate the circular logic at its core. The lying, cheating boyfriends are real; however, it's challenging to accept as true that you are *finding* this particular group of gay men because of what is going on inside of you.

If you have pejorative views of gay men, you can create self-fulfilling prophecies that will be incompatible with finding a mate. You may believe that there is "no one out there anymore" and find yourself not dating. You may believe that "all gay men abuse drugs " and become involved with men who are substance abusers and/or alcoholics. You may believe that "all gay men cheat" and find yourself dating men who are having clandestine affairs. And as indicated, you can *become* what you loathe because of this process.

The cycle can be stopped, however.

To do this, let's begin by looking at a story that illustrates one form of this problem.

Roy is a forty-six-year-old librarian living in New York City. He met Thomas, a thirty-nine-year-old teacher, also from New York, at a dinner party during Pride Week in June 2000.

Thomas had had a fourteen-year relationship that ended when his lover died of cancer in 1997. He went through a difficult period after that. He had been in love and his relationship had been an exceedingly happy one. It was a loss that cut into his heart and soul. He dropped out of sight and resolved never to date again. But gradually, with good support from friends and a willingness to accept the loss, he moved forward. By the time he met Roy he was ready to start over.

Roy's history is quite different. He never sustained a relationship more than a year, and had some bad experiences. One of his partners was a drug addict who ran up a $5,000 credit card bill in Roy's name. Years after they split up Roy was still paying back the money. Another experience was less dramatic but no less traumatic. His boyfriend Marshal announced to him one day, quite unexpectedly, that he was "not really ready for a relationship." They had been together eight months at that time and Roy was devastated.

For years, Roy had numerous one-night sexual liaisons. Roy was quite attractive and it was easy for him to meet men. But he was not satisfied with this. He felt lonely and empty, and desired a partner to share his life.

Roy was very excited when he met Thomas. Thomas was as intellectual as he was, and they both realized very early on that they had a lot in common. Although Roy felt very comfortable, he also had a nagging thought that "this was always what happened in the beginning."

Ten months into their relationship, some of the predictable stresses occurred. Both had been enmeshed and wanted to focus a little more on their individual lives. There were also some of the daily life hassles that were not particularly significant—Thomas was occasionally tired when they had a date, they preferred different kinds of restaurants, and they had minor quarrels about some social issues. But nothing was seriously wrong—both were honest, the sex was great, and they were in love. Nothing was seriously wrong—other than what was going on in Roy's mind.

When they reached a year together, Roy began feeling moody quite often. When Thomas asked him what was wrong, he'd say that he was "tired of his life" and wanted a "change." What he was specifically tired of and what he wanted to change he could not identify.

Roy grew more irritable. As Thomas tried to find out what was wrong, he became irritable with him. "Why can't you stop probing? Why can't you just leave me alone for a while?" he would thunder at Thomas. Thomas was very put off by this. In his mind, he was trying to be supportive and the thanks he got was to be yelled at.

After about a month of this, Roy began to "discover" what was wrong. It was Thomas. Anything he hadn't particularly liked about him before—from the shoes he wore to his politics about global warming—became unacceptable flaws. The aspects of Thomas that he loved—his warmth and sensitivity, among many other qualities—seemed somehow beside the point.

Thomas desperately tried to stop what he accurately perceived as their relationship nose-diving. When he tried to talk to Roy, Roy was too busy, too tired, or too uninterested. Thomas suggested they see a counselor and Roy laughed. "You see a counselor. You're the one who needs help."

On a rather rainy Sunday morning in late October, Thomas met Roy for lunch and informed him that he could no longer be with him. "I love you very much, but your behavior the past few months has been impossible. I don't know what on earth has happened, but I can't take this anymore."

"If you really loved me, you would stick by me," Roy responded. "Have a good life, Thomas."

Roy initially felt very relieved, as if a burden had been lifted. But his relief was peppered with thoughts of resentment and "confirmation" of what he "knew" all along: "Ran when the kitchen got too hot," he told himself. "Typical gay man."

A week later Roy started to feel different. His "relief" was replaced by a stinging void and a creeping suspicion that he had made a major life blunder.

He did. Let's take a look at what happened.

After some therapy, Roy recognized that he harbored some powerful beliefs of which hitherto, he was only dimly aware. He discovered that he had accepted as fact, *before he even met Thomas,* that a committed long-term relationship with another man was not possible. He further learned, to his dismay, that this *was the single most significant reason why it ended*—not because they weren't in love, not because there was any serious dysfunction. *Only a lethal self-fulfilling prophecy.*

Roy was more fortunate than others. He had the insight and motivation to seek help and find out what was really going on. Although he never went back with Thomas, there was hope he wouldn't repeat this scenario in the future.

A number of factors contributed to the development of these beliefs. Certainly his two hurtful experiences were significant. But long ago, when Roy was just a boy, he learned that gay relationships were "abnormal" and doomed. As an adult, he consciously understood that these ideas were homophobic thoughts derived from a negative attitude toward same-sex love. But that didn't really alter, on a deeper level, what he believed. His adult culture, even his gay friends, unwittingly played into this thinking. He knew many couples that "failed" but had little exposure to those whose relationships were working. When he'd get together with friends, they spent a lot of time discussing how men and relationships were so difficult. This kind of repetitive bitching helped reinforce Roy's negative expectations. Although such venting felt emotionally relieving in the short run, it also had the power, unbeknownst to him, to make his negative beliefs even more unyielding.

His history of one-night stands was also significant. Although he felt that he was doing this to bide time until Mr. Right came along, it affected his ability to be psychologically available for a committed relationship.

The tricking created an emotional void that buttressed his feelings about the impossibility of a gay relationship working out. His encounters were primarily alcohol enhanced, quick sex without any real human connection. The cyclic ritual of becoming sexually intimate within hours or even minutes of meeting someone had a way of debasing his feelings both about himself and the man he had just met. Roy felt himself and his prospective trick fraudulent, as they bestowed what he considered meaningless flattery upon each other in an effort to get laid.

Then along came Thomas, and Roy was required to make a 180-degree psychological shift. Although he desperately wanted to, he couldn't.

His mountain of negative beliefs *unconsciously* set the following scene: "The guy will appear nice at first but he will then turn out to be no good just like all the rest. *Inevitably, the relationship will not work.*"

When they reached the eighth month and this was clearly not happening, it actually caused a great deal of anxiety for Roy. If a prediction based on a strong belief does not occur, it can be unsettling—even if the belief is damaging. This is evident with chronic worriers—nothing is more disturbing to such people than to have nothing to worry about! Chronic worriers always find something. Roy "found" his prediction by becoming distant, angry, and blaming until *he finally provoked Thomas into leaving.* Initially, he felt relieved—his anxiety abated because the prediction had come true. Luckily, he had enough insight to recognize that something wasn't right. The healthier part of him questioned whether Thomas was really the problem.

There are a number of things you can do to prevent this kind of difficulty from interfering with your life before you even meet a potential partner.

Believe in Your Own Power

It's true that "shit happens." You could be walking along the street and (G-d forbid) part of a building could fall on you. You really had nothing to do with that. But, as said at the beginning of this chapter, a great deal of misery in life *is* self-inflicted. Recognizing that you hold the power is the first step in preventing its occurrence.

Of course you can't just order yourself to believe this. You'll need evidence. Start by looking at your own behavior. Writing about this in a journal may help but you could also think about it or talk with a trusted friend.

Does something seem to happen to you repeatedly that you don't want? Let's get away from boyfriends for a moment and look at other aspects of your life. Perhaps you don't get to appointments on time, or employment interviews seem to always go wrong, or you can't put together any kind of furniture, no matter how simple and clear the instructions. You may think of many other possible examples.

Consider what you believe about the experience and what behavior actually takes place.

For example, let's assume you have problems with being on time. Let's also assume you have concluded that you're simply a tardy person; you've been like this for as long as you can remember. If you monitor your behavior closely, however, you may discover that you consistently leave less time than necessary to get to engagements. The question is: why does this happen? Is there a gene that is causing this or are *you making behavioral choices?* Those choices could be (1) reading some mail that you "have to get to" as the clock is ticking away, (2) concluding there will probably be no traffic when nine out of ten times the freeway is jammed, or (3) forgetting to look at the clock and then all of a sudden discovering that it's later than you think. There could be other behavioral choices. The question you need to ask yourself is: does this "just happen" or is there some reason I am behaving in this manner?

The salient reason may be that you have labeled yourself "tardy."

We often live the labels we give ourselves because this creates comfort and order (no matter how equally unhelpful it may also be). As I indicated with Roy, if one strongly believes something (whether it's about oneself or something one expects from others) it's *reassuring* to experience life in line with that conviction, and disturbing to experience that which contradicts the belief. In relation to the tardiness example, this can happen to you because *you make behavioral choices that support the persona you know and are familiar with.* Although it certainly may cause problems, familiarity is comforting. It takes work to (1) question a strongly held belief, (2) consider the presence of a self-fulfilling prophecy and your role and power in it, (3) make the decision to craft different behavioral choices, and (4) accept initial discomfort with the unfamiliar.

If you can make peace with doing this work, you can create constructive life changes. This certainly applies to your problems with meeting the right kind of men. Do you tend to pick up guys who are drunk? Do you look for men almost exclusively in bars or clubs? Do you get interested when a guy tells you his lover is out of town and invites you home? Do you decide to date someone whom you've caught in a lie in the first ten minutes of speaking with him? Do you tell lies and exaggerations? Do you go out looking with the expectation that you're going to find a shithead?

These kinds of behaviors can be changed because they are choices. You don't have to pick up drunks and you can walk away from liars and cheaters. You certainly don't have to engage in that behavior yourself. You can question your expectations and refrain from going out when you are in a particularly foul "all men are pigs" mood. You can vary the places, times, and situations when and where you meet men. You don't have to sleep with anyone on a first encounter. You don't have to sleep with anyone until you're sure it's right for you.

Choosing *not to engage* in behavior that ends up kicking you in the ass is very empowering. Choosing *not to engage* in behavior that reinforces the belief that a good man and a viable relationship are impossible will change your life. You will find out that you really do have a choice, and that there can be a different, positive outcome for you. The man you've been looking for can enter your life.

But So Many Gay Guys Are Such a Mess!

Although you may understand the process as discussed, what if, in your heart of hearts, you still believe that too many gay men are too screwed up to form a committed, real adult relationship? Last week you found out that the guy you've been dating has a lover he forgot to mention. Your friend Santiago cheats on his boyfriend every time he visits New York. Every guy you've met in the past year has an alcohol, drug, and/or sex addiction. Kerry and Michael are calling it quits after five years—Kerry ran off with a twenty-year-old Hawaiian bimbo. You haven't been a saint yourself.

Real Problems and False Conclusions

We do, of course, have real troubles. Some gay men are immature, shallow, and incapable of a serious relationship. The question is not whether this occurs, but what conclusions you draw from it. *Dismissing the role of pervasive societal homophobia, attributing this to intrinsic psychopathology, assuming all gay men behave this way, and believing you are powerless to live differently is a grand mistake.*

People Are Flawed

Freud, *not* referring to gay men per se but to the state of the human race, once wrote, "I have found little that is good about human beings. In my experience, most of them are trash" (Miller, Duncan, and Hubble, 1997, p. 60).

Yeah, he actually said that!

Although I hope you don't share Freud's views on this, people do often disappoint us. We are fallible creatures, and we can be petty, jealous, dishonest, irritable, nasty, and probably a few thousand other pejorative adjectives.

Although you certainly need to be discriminating in your search to find a real life partner, it's important to look at how judgmental you are about people in general. You may feel that being critical means having high standards, but it can have a way of backfiring. Being overly judgmental can give you a generalized bitter feeling toward others. This will limit your prospective available partners because when the right guy does come along, you're likely to see his flaws and not his strengths. He will not gain access and your self-fulfilling prophecy will be created.

Being less judgmental doesn't mean you condone, like, or invite poor behavior. It certainly doesn't mean you pick a partner who behaves in this manner. It simply means that you avoid condemning people and instead try to find some understanding of why a person behaves in the manner he does.

Try taking the stance that we are all just trying to satisfy our needs and the route to this goal is different for all of us.

An obnoxious drunk, for example, may have serious problems with self-esteem, and getting loaded is his way of attempting to be accepted. A liar may have difficulties with assertiveness, and believe he can't directly ask for what he needs.

Once again, the primary beneficiary of being tolerant is *you*. Not only can it make you more likely to find the right man, but it can help you become less critical of yourself. You will be at ease, feel better about yourself, and that image will be discernable to others. By the way, if you also help the world become a little more friendly, what the hell? It's good and it doesn't cost you anything!

Reframing Your Past, Lousy Experiences

"Reality" is a virtual phenomenon shaped by our experiences. Your friend may view his partner's need to have time apart as normal. If you had an ex who deceived you, you may perceive this as an excuse to cheat.

If you have been traumatized in a former relationship, you are more likely to see the potential bad and dismiss the good. Walking into the dating scene with this mind-set is a prescription for creating a destructive, self-fulfilling prophecy.

The first step in addressing this problem is to *take seriously* your experiences of relationship trauma. We often laugh at the dreadful men who enter our lives as a way to disarm their toxic effect. This is a helpful means of coping. However, if you delegitimize just how destructive the experience was ("Oh, I'm over that"), you are less likely to be in touch with how it's affected your perceptions of potential boyfriends today. Traumas don't go away by "forgetting," and a bad experience with an ex may very well rise to the level of trauma. I would seriously consider exploring such an experience in a therapeutic environment such as a supportive gay men's group, or in individual psychotherapy.

Taking it seriously gives you the best chance to transcend the hold it may continue to have on you in the present.

Internalized Homophobia

Growing up in a society that is intolerant of same-sex love can have only harmful effects on us. Sometimes we take on and believe in behaviors that conform to the offensive stereotypes society has set for gay men. If you've come to believe that sexuality is the primary manner in which gay men are defined, you may view yourself and others as "tops" and "bottoms" rather than multidimensional human beings. If you believe that older gay men must wind up alone, lonely, and bitter, *if you strongly believe this,* tragically, you could find yourself in that place.

Anger and disgust of fellow gay men also grows from internalized homophobia.

Many beliefs are toxic. Among them are:

- all gay men are pigs—they will lie and cheat in order to get laid
- sex is all gay men want anyway
- being gay means you have to go to bars and dance clubs
- gay love is not normal or natural
- gay men are emotionally disturbed
- all gay men lie about sex
- over age twenty-five is over the hill
- all gay men need multiple partners
- two men can never work out
- gay men are emotionally immature
- gay men are not real men
- gay men are weak and disgusting
- gay men are evil and sinful

Most bigotry has some grains of truth. If you look hard enough, you may find "evidence" for some or all of this. The point is that it comes from a prejudicial dogmatist view based on a pathological societal phobia, not what real, living gay men are all about.

Psychopathology

There is no scientific evidence that gay men are any more psychologically disturbed than the general population. There is no empirical evidence supporting the pejorative attributes just listed (or the many others that could be easily added). Yet the notion that gay men are mentally ill is a belief that has been debunked in only relatively recent times.

There is plenty of blame to go around for the dissemination of these ideas. Unfortunately, a considerable amount of this can be pinned on the mental health community.

Psychiatry

One group principally responsible for propagating the belief that gay men are mentally ill or developmentally "arrested" is psychiatrists. Other mental health professionals, including my own profession of social workers, also share responsibility. I emphasize psychiatry because psychiatrists have the most power and are most closely aligned with the medical model. The medical model is the basis of ideas of normalcy and *pathology in relation to behavior.* Although it's beyond the scope of this book to exhaustively examine the connection between psychiatry and the psychopathological view, a few points are in order.

Same-sex love terrifies people for a variety of reasons, including the fear of diversity, the fear of a new definition of family, the challenge to traditional sex roles and sexism, and the discomfort with same-sex erotic feelings in those who consider themselves, or want to consider themselves, heterosexual.

Mental health professionals, similar to everyone else, are subject to these fears. Instead of defining this as a societal pathology (homophobia), they in a sense convert *their problem* (and society's) into a pseudoscientific explanation of homosexuality. They used their authority as "definers" of mental health and illness to support the prevailing homophobic cultural mores. Lots of the "proof" for their view came from anecdotal case studies of a skewed population of gay people in therapy tormented by their homosexuality and wanting to change. Of course, they didn't focus on the homophobic societal tyranny behind the desire to convert. From this they concluded that the entire gay population was psychologically fixated, had dominant mothers and distant fathers, and a whole ton of other malarkey. They not only succeeded in doing a first-class job of debasing us, but also slandered our parents; they were blamed for causing us to be "abnormal" and "sick." Elitist psychiatrists who hid behind "gatekeeper" roles to propagate their own and society's prejudices have injured countless gay men and lesbians, along with their mothers and fathers.

Although these fuddy-duddies seem pretty laughable by today's standards, what they did *and continue to do* (homosexuality is no longer defined as a mental disorder, but the idea still flourishes among some psychiatrists and other mental health clinicians) is no laughing matter. Pathologizing same-sex love puts the seal of scientific validity on the view that gay men and lesbians are grievously damaged. That's influential, far-reaching harm.

Despite the fact that society at large and the mental health field have come a long way in the past thirty years, this view still haunts the psyches of many of us in the gay community. It's imperative to challenge these thoughts, and to recognize that they are products of bigotry and fear, not science. If you or other gay men you know have emotional and/or other challenges of living, these difficulties exist because human beings experience these kinds of problems, not because you or they are gay.

So Where Are the Decent Gay Men?

The good news is everywhere. The challenge: you have to keep your eyes open and monitor your conclusions and perceptions.

Most of us know of and have been through bad situations in our past relationships—yet we consider ourselves upstanding and also have friends who are decent gay men. The obvious logic is that there are thousands, perhaps millions, of other gay men who are also decent.

Part of the problem is selective perception. Because of your history, coupled with pervasive homophobic messages as discussed, it may seem that there is "nobody out there." It's easy to recall people who are inappropriate and, conversely, difficult to think of fellows who have impressed you.

Another way this may operate is by dismissing men before you have given yourself adequate time to really get to know them. For example, when you detect flaws in people, which you inevitably will, you may think you've discovered unsuitability. It's very possible you have found only that the man is human. As mentioned previously, I certainly don't advocate getting involved with the wrong man. But I would be wary of instant, wholesale rejection the minute you detect imperfection. This sometimes happens when a sexual experience is less than heavenly, but it need not be sex. He could have said the wrong thing or arrived five minutes late, or have been in less than an exultant mood. Take inventory of what causes you to go into instant rejection mode. You may discover that you have rejected guys who may have been quite decent.

It's also possible you rejected guys not because of "imperfection," but because of something you didn't expect or something that didn't fit into your narrow criteria of acceptability. He may have been older, younger, shorter, heavier, smarter, not smart enough, richer, poorer, etc., than you wanted or first believed to be true. Think back. Have you rejected guys such as this? Did you perhaps act too hastily?

My point is not to have you lament over missed opportunities. It's to get you to realize that there are many decent gay men who could become your life partner.

Your Behavior

I firmly believe that what you give out is directly related to what you get. You may not see that immediately, but it has a way of happening in the long run. Try a little experiment. For one day, behave in a very friendly, happy manner to everyone you encounter. Say hello to the deli guy who makes you a sandwich. When someone helps you find something in the grocery store, say, "Thank you, sir" or "Thank you, madam." Smile at strangers. Smile to yourself.

Sure, not everyone will you react to you, but my prediction is that you will get a lot more positive feedback than you would get if you walked around in a dour or neutral manner.

Attracting decent men starts by behaving toward others in the way you want others to behave toward you. The great news about this is that you have the ultimate control in this arena.

It does not matter what you have done in the past. It certainly doesn't have to be governed by what you believe (erroneously what "everyone else is doing"). You simply have to decide what you want in a man *and then go out and act in the desired manner yourself!*

There are two very significant benefits to this. As mentioned, you will attract those who behave in the same manner. But more important, it will serve to disparage your belief about the dearth of men suitable for long-term, committed relationships.

Gay men are everywhere. Your potential, future partner is out there. But *meeting* him, even if he is literally in your face, requires more than just physical proximity. You have to have time and energy and psychological readiness. You must be open and willing to take a risk. You need to be in surroundings that are comfortable for you.

Are social events in the light of day better than bars and clubs? How do you mentally and physically prepare for a night out? What are the best places to meet men? Are there best places? Do online meetings ever work? How much time should you spend "hunting"?

In Chapter 9 we explore these and other questions. Develop an effective social life and you'll create a milieu conducive to meeting a life partner.

Chapter 9

Where Are the Men?
How to Have a Great Social Life

I feel it's possible to meet a potential partner in any environment in which you feel at ease.

Robert, forty-seven
Grocery Store Manager, Portland, Oregon

Ronnie lives in San Francisco, California. After being single for three years following a nine-year relationship, he was on a mission to find a boyfriend. He tried to be anywhere his prospective boyfriend might be. He went to bars and clubs each weekend. He never refused an invitation to a party. He joined an organization that arranged events to raise money for HIV programs. He met no one.

He became increasingly frustrated and tried even harder. He went out on "school" nights; he asked friends to fix him up; he talked to almost anyone on the street who didn't look psychotic (which was a little difficult in San Francisco). Still no boyfriend.

One Sunday morning, after a rather depressing Saturday night at the bars in the Castro, he brought a bag of pennies to Safeway to exchange them for dollars. The line was long. After waiting about twenty minutes, a man poured a large amount of coins into the machine and jammed it. Ronnie and the man in front of him began laughing and talking about what a mess this was turning into, and how much time it was taking. Ronnie was focused on the problem at hand and didn't think he was in the process of meeting someone. It only dawned on him when he and the man left Safeway and the man asked him if he'd like to have coffee at the Starbucks next door. I'll shorten the story. Ronnie has been with Joseph for almost a year now.

Attitude

Meeting your future lover begins by abandoning the idea that there are only certain places to come together. If you have an attitude of openness you can meet him anywhere. "Openness" means, foremost, that you have done your homework and you're psychologically ready to get involved. It means that you keep your senses receptive to possibilities without preconceived limitations. A conversation at a cocktail party is fine, but so is a conversation in the Laundromat. Ronnie was not thinking about romance, but fortunately said yes when Joseph asked him to coffee.

Openness also implies assertiveness. If you come across someone you'd like to meet, you have to be willing to take the initiative. If both of you are waiting for the other to make the first move, nothing may happen. I wonder how many potential relationships never begin because each man refuses to approach the other. Ronnie was lucky that Joseph stepped up to the plate. But I wouldn't rely on luck. *You* are more dependable than destiny.

Anywhere, Not Everywhere

Your future lover can be anywhere, but it doesn't mean he's everywhere. Some men eager to find a partner view every cute guy as their impending boyfriend. Grandiose planning such as this will communicate desperation and premature expectations. Most psychologically healthy men will take to the hills when they realize your agenda. Furthermore, your assessment skills are likely to be compromised. If he doesn't flee, you may find a boyfriend who becomes an ex-boyfriend once you return to earth and realize who he really is. The "everywhere" mind-set can lead to cynicism and defeat as the future lover repeatedly turns out to be "nowhere." You have to make peace with taking small steps and with the delicate balancing act *of being open to possibilities without expecting every encounter to lead somewhere.*

As part of a control crazed society, this will be difficult. When you meet someone who you think is a great guy, you can't help envisioning much more. The desire for control soon "plans and demands" that much more happen. You have to work at letting go of this tendency because it's as illogical as it is self-destructive. You don't really know someone you have just met, and you are even less knowledgeable about a future with him. At this juncture you need to *enjoy the moment* and work at discovering each other. If you're right for one another, this affords you the best prospect of a future together. In my experience, people who are immediately talking about a future often break up quickly.

Is This Work?

Just as in pursuit of any other important life goals, you have to plan and craft and do what it takes to get what you want in a life partner. To some degree it *is* work. But I am concerned about the pejorative notion associated with the word "work." It doesn't mean this has to be an arduous, painful task. As of a matter of fact, it's imperative that you relax and enjoy the experience. How do you do that? First, realize that attempting to meet someone is never a life-or-death endeavor. If you find someone interesting and he doesn't find you attractive, or for some other reason does not respond to you, so be it. In fact, you should expect this. You are going to be approaching lots of men and you can't expect that all of them will react positively.

Preparation

Looking for a partner means you have to involve yourself in the world. You must attend social functions. You need to be alert, maintain a positive mood, execute good social skills, and take emotional risks. You'll want to look, act, and feel your best. All of this requires energy. To state the obvious, you have to take good care of your body in order to do this. Eating well, getting plenty of rest and exercise, reducing anxiety and stress, and so on, is crucial.

The Journey and the Goal

View the journey and not just the goal as enjoyable. Meeting new people can be stimulating and exciting. Flirting is fun, sexy, and a turn-on. Sure, keep your eye on the prize, but there is value to more than just the prize.

Scorecards

Scorecards are great for baseball games but not for love searching. If getting a phone number is a "win" and meeting no one is a "wasted night," you're setting yourself up. View the act of socializing as a victory in and of itself. Not only can it be enjoyable in its own right, but being out there is what will create the opportunity for you to meet someone. Give yourself deserved credit for that.

Your Internal Critic

Be very aware of what your internal voice is saying. If that voice is very critical or defeatist, you're going to feel horrible.

An attempt or even ten attempts that go nowhere do not mean that the pursuit is futile. One of the most painful things you can tell yourself is that "I'm *never* going to meet anyone" or "this is just a waste, there's no one out there anymore." If your difficulties persist, you may have to examine your approach, or where you are looking, or some other variable. But the "never going to meet anyone" mind-set is mental poison and *not true.* I can tell you unequivocally, as a gay man and a psychotherapist, that there are scores and scores of gay men looking for lovers.

"Rejection" and the Internal Critic

Chapter 10 will address in detail the issue of rejection. But a few words are in order now. Men you approach who don't appear interested in you reveals very, very little. It says only that at the moment you approached that person, *for whatever reason* (and it could be that his hemorrhoids hurt, as well as not finding you attractive), he chose not to respond to you in the way you would have wanted him to respond. *It says nothing about you.* Some gay men who get rejected go on a mental orgy of self-reproach. They tell themselves that they were rejected because the man they approached found them too fat/thin/short/tall/old/young/whatever and that they *are* therefore too fat/thin/short, etc. This kind of thinking is outright psychological diarrhea because (1) you have no idea what someone is thinking unless you can read minds, and (2) what on earth does what someone think have *anything to do with who you are?* If you find yourself thinking in this manner, replace the thought with "lying mental poison," or "psychological diarrhea," or "shit on rye bread" (a Brooklyn expression), or anything else that will rid you of *false* and highly destructive ideas. As I said, more on this in the following chapter.

Balance

Looking for a lover should not consume your life. Spending almost all of your free time in this pursuit will be exhausting and yield diminishing results. Yes, it's a priority, but you have to strike a balance. Sometimes it's better to sit home in front of the television with pizza and chocolate chocolate chip Häagen-Dazs. It's OK to go out with friends and forget about looking for a man. It's fine to sit in a café with a book and not want to be bothered. As I matter of fact, I strongly suggest you do these and other activities that don't include trying to find a boyfriend. You may fear that you will miss an opportunity. Perhaps you will. But you are much more likely to forego a chance if you're obsessively on the prowl. That will make you tired and uptight. Any activity mandates breaks and time off. This is no different.

Anxiety

It's quite normal to be somewhat anxious when you are trying to meet others. However, if your anxiety becomes overwhelming it can interfere with socializing. If a glass of wine or a beer at a social event loosens you up a little, go ahead and have a drink (assuming you aren't an alcoholic or don't have other problems with alcohol). Obviously, if you need lots of alcohol or other chemicals to be able to approach people, this is not the way to deal with your anxiety.

A group therapy milieu focused on social anxiety can be helpful. In such a setting you can practice social behavior while addressing the cognitive components of your anxiety. For example, you can role-play initiating a conversation with a stranger. The group can then discuss their observations of your behavior, and you can tell them about thoughts that went through your head while you were doing the role-play. Most anxious thoughts are exaggerations with irrational, catastrophic images and notions. Thus, you may be thinking that your attempt to start a conversation resulted in you making a "total fool" out of yourself, and that your behavior was "shameful and embarrassing." The group members may see it very differently. They may report that you looked a little anxious or even perhaps *quite skillful*. This reality check can break your toxic, irrational thinking. Carrying out the actual behavior, especially with and in front of others in a supportive, safe setting, teaches you, experientially, anxiety reduction.

You approach a stranger to initiate a conversation, others watch, and nothing terrible happens. Your less anxious feelings can then be generalized to the real world.

A group setting can also teach you that others have some of the same fears as you do and help you to feel less strange and different.

You can also observe constructive social behavior modeled by the group leader or by other members. You may gain new social skills, which will help you to reduce anxiety and to feel more confident.

Some form of relaxation exercise before or during social encounters may be also be helpful. One very simple way for you to relax on the spot is to take slow, deep abdominal breaths (Bourne, 1995). There are many good books and tapes that teach relaxation exercises, and I strongly recommend them. Relaxation exercises can be a good adjunct to group or individual therapy.

Where Can You Meet Men?

Virtually any environment is potentially a place to meet men. Nevertheless, some settings, including cyberspace, are either specifically designed for more conducive to meeting other gay men. Which is right for you?

I'd like to begin by questioning the holy grail of thought that "bars don't work" and "joining a gay organization" does. Often those who are burnt out on bars and clubs conclude that this is the answer. Get out of the dark, alcohol-laden pits and into the light of an organization! One of the arguments is that alcohol is the only common denominator in a bar. Organizations bring together those who have common interests. Join a gay hiking club, for example, and you'll find other gay men who like hiking.

Sounds good on paper. But I believe that is a very simplistic view of a much more complex phenomenon.

You may have hiking in common, but that says nothing of the multitudinous other variables necessary to create a viable relationship. When you set yourself up in this manner, you can become quite unenthusiastic about organizations in general once the boyfriend is not found. What's even more problematic about this viewpoint is that it diminishes the role of *you*. The environment becomes the salient variable. That's a mistake. Your calm demeanor, positive attitude, readiness to become involved, good social skills, and willingness and ability to be assertive are the elements that are going to find you a man.

That being said, environments do impact us. Different places and situations have rules and expectations specific to the setting. Let's try to understand this and see how you can use that knowledge to your benefit.

Comfort

To begin with, your comfort is vital. Surroundings that put you at ease will be the places where you will shine. Obviously, if your comfort zone is very limited, it's sound logic to work on expanding it. However, to put yourself in places you truly don't want to be in makes no sense—that means *wherever* you're ill at ease, including bars and clubs. These establishments are the most publicized places in our community, but they're not for everyone, and not everyone goes there. Honor your wishes. It's a good way to begin this journey because you're setting an affirmative tone. You're validating the importance of taking care of yourself first and foremost.

Online

Online is a very convenient way to meet men that presents you with a great deal of choice. From chat rooms to instant messaging to databases of others seeking relationships, you can find lots of men any time of day or night.

Sitting at a computer is easy. You don't have to shower and put on nice clothes. There's no significant risk of social shame because you can remain anonymous. Saying hello is smooth and anxiety free. If the conversation goes nowhere, he's gone with a click. If you don't like his picture, you can delete it. All of this expediency comes with a price.

The immense choice and facility of instantly clicking someone out of your awareness tends to degrade the real people represented on the screen. If he has a mole you don't like or he's five years older than you prefer, he's gone. Move on to the next one.

The virtual world may seem a candy store of endless opportunities that you can revel in until the perfect guy appears, but that's a mirage. The kind of activity I just described treats people as objects, not humans. Objectifying people means denigrating their worth, which means you really can't feel good about them. The men on your screen are doing the same to you. This is unlikely to produce the beginning of a relationship. More probable, an endless, frustrating search to find the perfect guy ensues, as suitable men are passed over.

It doesn't have to be this way. You can behave toward people online as you'd relate to them if they were in front of you. If you don't want to engage with someone, be tactful and polite. Tell him you're not interested and wish him luck. More important, think twice about wholesale rejection and searching for the perfect man. Give others and, more important, *give yourself* a chance. If you behave in this manner online, you're more likely to avoid obsessive searching, feel good about the people you meet, and increase the likelihood of finding someone suitable for you.

Virtual Is Not Real

A virtual relationship needs to become, eventually, a tangible one if you want a flesh-and-blood boyfriend. This means the normative anxiety and diminished control in a real-life situation must be addressed. If your computer has been serving to protect you from this, it will be unnerving when you realize that it has only been postponing this process. Furthermore, problems with social interaction and anxiety will be worsened by the social avoidant quality of the computer.

If however, the computer doesn't take the place of a real social life, it can be a great adjunct to other venues for meeting men. One way to guarantee this is to be aware of how much time you spend online versus how much time in real social settings. If you are hooked on the computer, you have to take responsibility for unhooking yourself.

Dishonesty

The online environment is notoriously deceitful. People represent themselves to be what they are not. They send pictures that are ten years old, inaccurately describe their physical characteristics, lie about who they are and what they do and so on. Many people are very disappointed once they meet the person they have been e-mailing or chatting with.

It's important to be aware of this without concluding that *everyone* you meet online is a liar. You can tell a virtual acquaintance that if he is not who he is when you meet, he's wasting his time. Some guys just want to keep a virtual relationship. One way to test this is to ask to meet within a relatively short period of time. If you want a real life partner, and he wants an online fantasy, it's best you find this out ASAP. Finally, but probably foremost, you must be honest. It may be fun for you to be someone you are not, but that will not fare well once you meet the man. Honesty is a cardinal requisite in any viable relationship. If you are lying before you even meet, any potential for a future is very low.

Bars and Clubs

Bars have a long history in our community. They served as a sort of safe haven from homophobic subjugation. Out in the world you had to hide your identity, but in a bar you could be yourself. Of course they were not totally safe. This may seem hard to believe if you're young, but the man on the next stool whom you tried to pick up could be a police officer who could arrest you. The police also frequently raided bars, and no raid is more famous than the one that occurred at The Stonewall, resulting in riots and the birth of the modern gay rights movement (Duberman, 1993). Bars (for brevity I will use the term "bars" to refer to all forms of bars including large dance clubs) continue to provide an important social milieu for our community. In large cities there are scores of bars catering to numerous interests.

Bars can be an excellent place to meet others. From low-key neighborhood bars that resemble "Cheers," where everybody knows your name, to places catering primarily to specific crowds such as the leather community, to video bars and collegiate bars and large clubs, bars serve an important social function for all segments of our community. Certain bars may be "cruisey" whereas others are places you go with friends, but they are all designated social settings with social rules and expectations that facilitate meeting others. Bars are set up to allow people to relax, have a drink, kick back, talk to others, etc.

Bars also create a physical environment that encourages socializing. You'll often find a pinball machine and/or a pool table. Music usually plays. Many show videos. A party atmosphere is created. Alcohol is available and *light* drinking can be disinhibiting and help ease social interaction. Some bars have baseball teams, which is another way they encourage meeting others. Some bars have dancing, and large clubs usually have sizable dance areas. Dancing is a great forum for socializing. It can be very sexy, and it's a way to observe others and to be observed. Dancing is also fabulous exercise, and it can help you feel mentally and physically fit. This, in turn, can only facilitate meeting others. Dancing also creates a cheerful atmosphere. Watch others on the dance floor and you will see lots of smiles. Smiling and laughing is infectious.

Of course, bars also have their share of problems.

To a large degree, particularly with cruise bars, physical appearance is primary. This will be addressed in detail in Chapter 10. Bars can be a meat market based on very superficial criteria. People who don't fit the bill get rejected. They may leave alone and feel discontented. Ironically, guys who "score" often wind up unhappy also. Why? A friend of mine by the name of Brendan had an expression that will answer this: "Last night's trick is tomorrow's nightmare." If physical appearance is the only or primary criterion—and if you're toasted when you meet—your honey of the night may look like Igor in the morning. His witty banter may now sound asinine, your thoughts that he could be your next boyfriend, ludicrous.

> Usually what I hear is that people are trying to turn a trick into a boyfriend, which doesn't ever really work very well. . . . It's about objectification. (It's about) having sex with body parts instead of a person.
>
> Brian Wolfe, MFT
> Private Practice, San Francisco, California

Obviously, meeting guys in this manner is not a way to begin a relationship. If you're looking for love, a fast lay has a way of interfering with that goal. Thinking with your dick not only makes you disregard other characteristics that may be incompatible with what you're looking for, but it has a way of demeaning, in your mind, the person you just screwed. Sexual freedom and the sexual revolution aside, people you have sex with right away tend to be seen as "tricks," as opposed to husband material. Most of us in American society have deeply ambivalent feelings about sexuality. When we consummate sex with a person we've just met, that person becomes devalued. Is this rational? Of course not! But it's how countless gay men operate. Although nothing is qualitatively different about a "trick," this mind-set creates a truth that forecloses opportunities. If you and the man you've slept with can surmount this thinking, a relationship is possible. Some unions begin this way. However, this attitude is deep-seated, and, in my experience, tricks turning into life partners is rare.

Of course no law says you must go home immediately with a guy you meet in a bar. Take his number and get to know him uninfluenced by the horniness of the moment, and the drugs and/or alcohol. If he doesn't want to do this, or if he agrees only to never materialize again, you found out he's not a potential partner without wasting a lot of time.

I mentioned earlier that light drinking may be helpful because it can be mildly disinhibiting. Unfortunately, many people do *a lot* of drinking. Drug use is also quite widespread, particularly in big clubs.

Substance abuse and excessive drinking are complex behaviors that I make no pretense of examining in any significant way. To the extent that they affect meeting a life partner, I can say this: these serious problems will only interfere with your pursuit. If you have any questions whether your drinking and/or drug usage is excessive, that is reason enough to consult a mental health professional who has training in this area.

Booze and chemicals (excessive use of) will not only make you unattractive to others who are seeking a healthy relationship, they can seriously impede your judgment and bring men into your life who aren't good for you. They can compromise your health, your future, and even your survival. Should you somehow find and fall in love with the right man despite this problem, sooner or later it will drive a wedge between the two of you. When alcohol and/or other chemicals are in the picture, it's either them or the relationship. They cannot co-exist.

Some people in recovery will not frequent bars, and that is a perfectly reasonable decision. Not only do they find them dangerously tempting, but even if they don't succumb the experience is stressful and uncomfortable. Others can feel at ease and do not experience this conflict. If you are in recovery, discuss this with your counselor(s). Just because you feel confident doesn't mean the environment couldn't be detrimental to your recovery.

If you happen to be someone who is simply not into drinking or drugs, bars may not be right for you. You may feel out of step with some of the partying around you. On the other hand, many people can enjoy bars without using alcohol and/or drugs. It's relatively common these days to see guys in bars carrying bottled water. It's your choice. Just make certain you feel comfortable.

Smoke, Noise, and Crowds

In California, where I live, smoking is prohibited in all bars and clubs. This is the exception rather than the rule in most of the United States at the time of this writing. The dangers of secondhand smoke have been well documented. Smoke also leaves an odor on your skin, hair, and clothing. If you're a nonsmoker and you find this offensive, bars are simply not the place for you to be.

Bars often (but not always) mean loud music, dim lights, and large numbers of people. To some, this creates a feeling of community, togetherness, sexual stimulation, and relaxation; for others, just the contrary. Being unable to move freely, banging into others, and fearing for one's safety in the event of an emergency (which may be a very real concern) can be the antithesis of a fun night out. If this is how you feel, don't try to force yourself to enjoy it. It's not for you and there is nothing wrong with that. There are many other ways to meet guys.

The volume level in many bars makes talking difficult if not impossible. There is also a real concern about hearing loss. Dim lights tend to cause people to look better than they really appear. Screaming in order to communicate, and having a nasty surprise when you see your prospective interest in brighter light, is not what some call amusing.

Large crowds can also be very stressful. Masses of people create an aura of social disengagement. When you're in such an environment, you are likely to experience a significantly decreased sense of intimacy. Some people endure a feeling of being lost, irrelevant, and invisible.

Large numbers can make initial connections more difficult in another way. Because there are so many men and so much stimulation, some guys find it hard to "settle." They think someone "better" may come along at any moment. If they do engage in a conversation, they keep their other eye, simultaneously, on the crowd. This can be insulting to the man they're conversing with, and frustrating and destructive to themselves. This "candy store" absorption usually has a way of backfiring. One winds up meeting no one.

Bars provide many ways to meet men but also create considerable challenges. Going to them, and the frequency you do, are decisions you have to make for yourself. The bottom line is that this is a setting you need to like if you want it to be a medium in which to meet potential life partners.

Sex Clubs

Bathhouses and other sex club-type establishments have "demand characteristics" or environmental expectations that are incompatible with starting a relationship. The purpose of these places is to provide swift, multiple sexual contacts with no strings. Part of the enjoyment of this experience is to remain anonymous and forego any relatedness other than carnal gratification. Men often don't speak in these places, let alone exchange numbers and make plans for dinner.

I see no problem in occasionally involving oneself in these activities. Even when you're actively seeking a relationship, sometimes it's OK to skip a night and just take care of business.

If you're a frequent flyer, however, and want to find a partner, you may be working against yourself. The heart of what makes sex clubs fun, aside from the easily available carnal indulgence, is the divestiture of "precourting" behavior—those awkward, exciting, and nerve-wracking attempts to get to know someone. But that's requisite for starting a relationship. You can't go from dick sucking to a drive in the country without saying something! If sex clubs become your modus operandi for socializing, you face two significant dilemmas. The atmosphere is a set up for not meeting anyone. More problematic is adopting the habit of sex without any other human connection. This can rust your social skills while increasing your anxiety of approaching men in alternative venues.

Sometimes an enthusiasm for sex clubs and other forms of anonymous sexual activity means you have a sexual addiction. As with substance and alcohol abuse, sex addiction is a complex problem that is beyond the scope of this book to address. Suffice it to say that sex addiction is incompatible with finding a healthy relationship. As with chemicals and booze, if you're questioning whether you have a problem, it's prudent to consult with a mental health professional qualified to assess and make recommendations.

All of this being said, it's not *impossible* to meet a lover in a sex club. There are often areas to take a break, have a soda, and mingle. Bathhouses have private rooms that can be conducive to conversation. It is not unheard of for two guys to begin talking in a public sex area and go off by themselves. Although I wouldn't recommend this setting as a great place to find a partner, *don't decide you can't just because it's a sex club.* If you encounter someone you think you'd like to get to know, *go ahead and break the goddamn social rule and start speaking to him!* Sure, you're risking a little embarrassment (he may not respond; someone may go *"shhhh"*), but what the hell? He could be your next boyfriend. Risking embarrassment is better than letting an opportunity pass you by.

Classes and Workshops

Attending adult classes is an excellent way to stimulate your mind, improve on or learn new skills, and meet potential life partners.

All courses are not created equal, however.

To begin with, if you want this to be a forum to meet other gay men, there have to be other gay men in the class. Obviously, there's no litmus test to determine this.

In some very openly gay communities, such as San Francisco, it's really difficult to be in any setting that *doesn't* have some gay men. But not everyone lives in San Francisco.

Some courses specifically cater to gay men, such as a gay history course or a gay male relationship course. If you don't have these classes in your area, you could always propose something similar to your local community college. Gender study education is a much-needed and increasingly acceptable part of education. Educators in your area may be very open to this suggestion.

Whatever class you take, it should provide a medium in which people can get to know one another. Any class that has student interaction and some level of personal revelation can be helpful. For example, as a writer, I have taken a number of short-story writing classes.

These classes are very student interactive. Writing short stories and reading them to the class inevitably reveals part of oneself. The same is true with an acting class. Learning thermodynamics (whatever that is) probably won't! Sharing oneself, even in a limited way, is how you and others get a sense of one another. If you like what you hear, you may want to take it further and ask the fellow out for coffee.

The great news is that adult education is very widespread and there are classes that address almost any interest. From how to make your dreams work for you to assertiveness training to speaking to the dead, they're out there. Often these classes last only one evening, which means little commitment and low cost.

Organizations

There are a plethora of organizations that you can join. Organizations, generally speaking, indicate interactions with others. I say "generally speaking" because if you volunteer for an association where you sit in an office by yourself manning the phones, you're not likely to meet many others.

As GLBT (gay, lesbian, bisexual, and transgender) liberation has come into its own, the number of clubs and associations throughout the country has become almost limitless. Furthermore, you don't have to restrict yourself to "gay organizations" as long as you can be assured that other gay men will be there.

Many cities and towns have gay directories. You can also search online for gay organizations or other kinds of groups in your area.

As mentioned, however, organizations are not necessarily the "answer" because even if you find someone with similar interests relative to the organization, it doesn't mean you will have *other* similar interests. That being said, joining an organization is still an excellent way to get to know others.

I would suggest focusing on organizations in which socializing is the main objective. Certainly you can meet someone while working together for a common cause, but a group whose aim is to meet others is congruent with your goals. Such organizations have parties, sports events, trips, and so on, and they are great ways to get to know others.

If there are no organizations such as this in your area, or you don't fancy what there is, why not start one? Think of something that particularly interests you (let's say gay men into local hiking), give the club a jazzy name, and then start telling the world about it. You can arrange a potluck as the first meeting and then discuss with the attendees what ideas they have and what to do next. Tell your friends about it, post it online, print out flyers, etc.

This is a merely a microfraction of the numerous ways you can create, promote, and grow a club. Outer space, not just the mere sky, is your limit!

Parties

Parties are wonderful ways to meet others. Similar to bars and clubs in a sense, they tend to be more intimate. Parties are specifically set up to relax, have fun, and meet and mingle with others. The "demand characteristics" of this situation clearly foster socializing.

Perhaps you don't get invited to many parties. What can you do about this? For one thing, let others know you're available. If you have a busy life, others might not invite you in the belief that you're unavailable. If you have a history of declining invitations, make a commitment to change that, and then let others know about your change.

Maybe your friends simply don't put together parties. What can you do? Make the party yourself (enlist a friend or two to share in the work and cost). Tell your friends to bring their friends and those friends to bring other friends.

Your Friends and Co-Workers

Sometimes one of the best sources for meeting potential partners is your friends or others whom you know.

Many of us shy away from the thought of being "fixed up." We think of this as contrived, desperate, and doomed to failure. But a person who is familiar with you and a potential match for you may be in a good position to judge a fit.

You do have to let others know that you are available, however. Many guys are uneasy with this. They feel embarrassed that they're alone and don't want to look needy. They keep their quest for love, something common to most human beings, a secret.

This is as irrational as it is self-destructive. If you want to meet someone, the world should know you're looking. As mentioned previously, passing up life-changing opportunities is far worse than temporary discomfort. What's particularly sad about missed chances is that you'll never know what you missed.

Letting the world know you're available doesn't mean you have to beg others to find you a man. Friends whom you are close with should simply know that this is a priority. If they are acquainted with or come across someone who they think is right for you, they should let you know about that person. How you get to meet him depends on the specifics of the situation. Perhaps they can have a get-together and invite the both of you. Others, such as co-workers, should know that you're in the process of looking. If someone whose judgment you trust offers to introduce you to someone, get introduced. What is the worst that can happen? You'll have a bad hour or two? So what? If you're worried about office gossip, let that go. People who gossip are in search of a *life* and you should feel sorry for them. Your goals, not your fears, should govern what you do.

Many Other Places and Situations

I have mentioned in the preceding pages but a fraction of the ways you can meet men. You can find your life partner in a café, the library, at the gym, while waiting to have your car washed, at work, sitting next to you on an airplane, at a bus stop, in the supermarket, at a funeral, and anywhere else people assemble. Keeping your eyes open, looking directly at people, smiling, feeling relaxed, and conveying confidence in speech and body posture will begin connections that can lead to a relationship.

The only problem is that being calm and confident is a formidable task for many. Why? Because rejection is intensely feared. You might smile and he may look away. You may start talking and he may walk. You may ask for his number and he may refuse. You may invite him out and he may be "busy"—for the next seventy years!

Rejection isn't comfortable, but how has it become the Frankenstein's monster of social intercourse? Why do people place so much stock in the acts and opinions of strangers? Why does it feel so personally insulting? How can you diminish this fear and free yourself to go after what and whom you want in your life?

We are going to address these questions in Chapter 10. Fear of rejection can be quite paralyzing and can cause you to miss out on a lot.

The man of your dreams can slip though your life if you're too terrified to approach him. He may feel the same, and so the relationship that could have been may never be. That shouldn't happen, especially when fear of rejection is an illogical anxiety that can be ameliorated once you explore it.

Chapter 10

Facing Rejection

When I was in my twenties (in the fifth century), I desperately wanted to meet a cute guy that I had seen around town. I lived in the Village in New York City at the time, and I often saw this guy in a bar called The Ninth Circle. He was kind of tall, with clear, soft-looking skin, an adorable smile, and straight, thick, light brown hair. He was Mr. Perfect for me, but the more I wanted to meet him, the more frightened I became. How could little old me walk up to such a perfect specimen of God's creation? What would I say? What if he wouldn't like me? He could be ten feet away from me, but walking up to him was like crossing the Red Sea without the help of Moses.

One fine weekend I was at a party, and who was standing in the living room by himself but my dream man—*all by himself.* The party was relatively small, and I knew I had to approach him or forever hold my peace! But I was jammed up with anxiety, so I decided to call on my friend *Bud Weiser.* I had one, and then another one, and then . . . well, who knows how many? Finally, with my heart still in my throat, I walked over to him and started to talk. My speech was slurred and it was difficult to understand me. I even had difficulty understanding me! He was polite, but expressed no interest.

I never tried to meet him again. I don't know if he would have been attracted to me had he not met me when I was intoxicated. But I know this: my fear of him rejecting me, and the crazy way I tried to "medicate" that fear, was certainly not helpful.

What Is Rejection to You?

When someone you want doesn't want you, what does this mean for you? How you respond to that is the heart of what will govern your feelings and behavior. If it means next to nothing, for example, you will feel about the same. If it means you're a "reject," your confidence will be shattered and your assertiveness paralyzed.

Most of us probably fare somewhere between these two poles. I can say with confidence, however, that many gay men have considerable difficulty with rejection.

Why So Much Difficulty?

There are multiple factors that cause the "fear of rejection" to be such an issue for gay men.

One has to do with the real negative responses we've had to endure growing up in a homophobic society. Many of us were rejected by other boys, male siblings, teachers, clergy, and our parents, particularly our dads. For some gay men rejection is a hot button, an unhealed wound that triggers long-standing feelings of shame and unacceptability. If that describes you, it's important to come to terms with how these feelings arose. That means you need to explore, understand, and ultimately transcend the hold these emotions continue to have on you today. Working this through in a group with other gay men may be an effective way to achieve this. Individual psychotherapy may also be helpful.

Fear of rejection is also related to a collective "need" to be approved by others. This is true for many people, heterosexual and gay, with or without any particular childhood struggles around feelings of inadequacy. Thus it's a common issue, but not necessarily a rational one.

In fact it's quite irrational. In a sentence, whatever your past was or was not, whatever is going on in your life presently, *fear of rejection makes absolutely no sense.* Once you can accept as true that *this worry is based on a material schism with reality,* it's going to be very difficult to fear rejection. In fact, you won't even dignify the issue with that word.

The Word Is Absurd

The old childhood rhyme my mom taught me—"Sticks and stones can break my bones but names will never harm me"—is, unfortunately, false. Words can be lethal. They are particularly destructive when we use them liberally without paying attention to their actual meaning. I should say "consciously paying attention," because our brains have a way of paying attention, even when we are not particularly aware of nor concerned about the literal connotation of a word. If the word is noxious, it can have only harmful consequences.

Let's say you often call yourself "stupid" when you make a mistake. If brought to your attention, you may laugh it off and say that you don't mean it literally. However, when faced with tasks or situations that present challenges, you are likely to believe you're not capable of succeeding and will either fail or avoid the problem altogether.

According to *The Oxford American Dictionary* (1980), to reject is "to refuse to accept, to put aside or send back as not to be chosen or used or done, etc." When you say you have been rejected, this is what you are telling yourself: you have been refused acceptance, put aside, sent back, not chosen, and not used. You may laugh, but this is what your brain is reading. Overcoming your fear of rejection begins by taking serious issue with this word.

No one, particularly a stranger, has the ability or authority or power to *decide anything about you, for you, or who you are as a person.* When you tell yourself that you've been rejected, you are bestowing upon the individual who rejected you an entitlement that is frankly absurd.

A person not demonstrating interest in you is communicating something about himself but *nothing* about you. He may reject you because *he finds* you physically unattractive, or for a multitude of other reasons that may have zero to do with how you appear. Whatever the grounds, his lack of interest in you is a process going on within himself. *It's his process; he owns it.* Perhaps he doesn't find you attractive, and it's because he likes short guys and you're tall. You and all the other tall guys in the world do not become unattractive by dint of this person's preferences. *His reasons cannot magically transform into your problem.*

This is not semantics. What I may consider God's gift to the male species you may find unexciting if not categorically hideous. Have you ever had this kind of an experience with a friend? If you have, probably each of you labeled the other's taste "crazy." You *each perceived* the hunk/troll differently based on your individual preferences. "Drop-dead gorgeous" or "hideous" was about you and your friend's perceptions, *not about the man you were observing.*

Although rejection in the context of someone not demonstrating interest in you is a misuse of the word as just described, for brevity I will still use it in this section.

Mind Reading

Many of us view rejection as disapproval of the way we look. In a meat market situation, this may be accurate. On the other hand, you really don't know what another person is thinking. He may not respond to your overtures because he's shy, anxious, lacks social skills, is not very verbal, is not in the mood to talk at that moment, is with someone, or is having stomach cramps! Analyzing why someone doesn't show interest is a waste of time and has a high likelihood of creating unwarranted blame. "I look like shit" or "he's just too stuck up" may be your conclusions. That's negative energy based on lack of information, which can only do you harm. If someone is uninterested, just accept it at face value (he's not responding for unknown reasons) and move on.

"Passive Rejection"

Some gay men expect to be approached and consider it "rejection" when it doesn't happen. With all due respect to those who believe this, that kind of thinking borders on lunacy. A man you want to meet may be thinking the same thing. If someone doesn't make the first move, nothing will happen. It's like driving. (Let me explain this analogy—I'm not crazy.) If you want to arrive home alive, *you* have to take responsibility for safety on the road and drive defensively. Likewise, if it's *your* goal to find a life partner, you have to take responsibility to make it happen. If you become partners, you can tell him later on what a sorry jerk he was for not smiling first. But right now, you have to initiate the process.

Low Self-Esteem and Rejection

Those who feel bad about themselves, who feel they don't "measure up" to others, will have the most difficulty with rejection. Such people view rejection as confirmation of their negative views of themselves. This is not logical thinking but neither is believing that you're unacceptably flawed or "less than" others. Having low self-esteem can also create a damaging vicious cycle, and a self-fulfilling prophecy. People with low self-esteem often communicate this to others both by what they say and how they carry themselves. Although they may not intend this on a conscious level, they are in effect saying to others, "I am not worth much." Others respond to this. They find themselves not attracted to such persons, sometimes not even realizing why.

If you suffer from low self-esteem, I suggest you seek professional help. Low self-esteem is impervious to the social environment. No amount of praise or acceptance will change how you feel. Low self-esteem comes from very deep-seated beliefs and they must be addressed. Indeed, if the scenario I described in the previous paragraph *doesn't* happen, you will still feel bad. You may believe that *not* being rejected was just a fluke, and wait around until the next opportunity for your belief to be "confirmed." Low self-esteem creates significant problems in formulating and maintaining healthy relationships.

General Irrational Ideas

Those of us who fear approaching others in social situations are often engaged in "self-talk" that is illogical, painful, and socially inhibiting. Let's examine some of this thinking and why it's nonsensical.

I couldn't walk up to him . . . we're not in the same class (of physical attractiveness).

This is one I told myself. Not only is this terribly subjective (how are "classes" of beauty defined and by whom—the Federal Beauty Committee?), but where is it written that people have to be equally attractive on some mythical scale in order to connect? You're breathing and he's breathing—that's all you need in common.

This is a party of beautiful people. I don't fit in.

Pretty much the same as the preceding thought. The Federal Beauty Committee doesn't exist. This group of strangers has not taken a vote and declared you persona non grata. You have as much right to be there as anyone else.

He's talking to others. I couldn't just walk over.

If you're able to walk, you can walk up to a group and introduce yourself. We sometimes feel that there's an invisible barrier around others who are talking. This is actually an internal psychological barrier we are carrying. Indeed, a group discussion is most likely formulated by different members joining in at different times. You can do the same. Simply walk up and when there's a pause in the conversation, say hello and introduce yourself. What's the worst that can happen? Are they going to scream, *"Go away, outsider, this is our conversation"*? I doubt that. If they do, they have a much bigger problem than you have!

He's not looking at me. He's definitely not interested in me.

Looking can take microseconds, so just because you didn't catch him looking at you doesn't mean he isn't watching. Since many of us are concerned that others may not return a cruise, we often gaze at warp speed.

There is also a phenomenon called selective perception. He may be looking but you don't see it. Have you ever had the experience of a friend telling you that you're being cruised and you think he's hallucinating? If you accept as true that very attractive men "just couldn't be interested in you," such a man may be gawking and you would still be wondering why you never meet men like him!

Furthermore, not looking doesn't necessarily mean not interested. He may simply not see you. He may not stare at others in general. He may be self-conscious. Find out what's going on. Walk up to him.

Everyone is talking and laughing and looking so comfortable. I'm a nervous wreck. I'm different.

Scores of people are anxious and unsure in social gatherings. Certainly it doesn't seem this way when you look at a large group and see people talking and laughing. But consider this: You can't see inside their heads, and you're looking from the vantage point *of an individual at a group*. When others "look out" from the group they are seeing the same thing and you are then part of that "relaxed," happy assemblage.

Walking over to someone is so obvious. Everyone will know I'm trying to pick him up. When they see he's not interested, they'll all be laughing.

As if others have nothing better to do than keep your actions under surveillance! People at social gatherings are there to meet other people. Their attention is focused on that and not on your anxieties. What you perceive as public shame is in all likelihood utterly invisible to others. Should someone actually be watching and "laughing" at you, consider that the poor fellow is in serious need of a life.

What if he's with someone? I would just die of embarrassment when that guy returns.

Watch that word "die." People die of heart attacks, cancer, and kidney failure. I've never known embarrassment to be fatal. But your unconscious can interpret that word as a primal danger and instruct you to avoid approaching the man at all costs. The outcome: you were never in danger of dying, but you're in real danger of missing a potential opportunity.

If he is with someone, perhaps that someone is just a friend. Indeed, when his friend comes back, you'll have the chance to meet him also. You've just now gained the opportunity of meeting two guys by approaching one. Some lovers have met by first meeting their partners' friends.

Should he be with someone and that someone does turn out to be his boyfriend, so what? Social gatherings are about meeting people and that's what you were trying to do. Just like everyone else is trying to do at this gathering. Just like these two boyfriends did at one point. Certainly it feels uneasy and disappointing if you discover that a guy you've been looking at has a boyfriend, but instead of being down on yourself, give yourself credit for trying.

Making Peace with Rejection

It's very likely, indeed certain, that some people you want will not want you. If you are serious about finding a partner, and are interacting with many men, the law of averages tells you that there will be guys you approach who will not be interested. Instead of viewing this as a failure, consider it part of the normal, expected outcome of social interaction. In fact, a considerable number of "rejections" means you are there and trying. That's good.

Making Peace with Discomfort

> . . . most humans don't really grow unless there's some pain involved. If you don't want to have to put up with any sort of pain or you can't tolerate any sort of pain, then what is your potential for growth?
>
> Brian Wolfe, MFT
> Private Practice, San Francisco, California

Socializing can and should be great fun. But when we attempt to make connections and they don't work out, there's no getting around the fact that it is not fun. We are a pain-avoidant society, and pain is often circumvented at all costs. However, you can't do that if you're seriously looking for a relationship. It's very important *not* to think of socializing as a pain-laden experience. That is inaccurate and will take all of the joy out of meeting people. On the other hand, there will be some uneasiness at times. Expecting and accepting that will make your "relationship" with rejection all the more uncomplicated.

The Word "Rejection"

As pointed out earlier, the word literally makes no sense because no stranger has the power to do this to you. Become very aware of the use of this word, particularly in your internal chatter. For example, right after a guy tells you he wants to "walk around, see you later" and you feel uncomfortable, get in touch with what you're telling yourself. As difficult as it may feel, remind yourself that you are disappointed and wish it could have turned out different *but this guy has no power to do anything to you.*

Remember You Can't Mind-Read

Someone who doesn't want you has his reasons, and you will probably never find them out. It makes literally no sense to get into an internal dialogue about what went wrong. It's like the debate about how many angels can dance on the head of a pin. He wasn't interested—it's over, move on. Life is too damn short to get involved with mental diarrhea.

Logic Can Make You Feel Good

Consider the following vignette.

Rex finally approached a man he had been looking at for a half hour. At times the man had been looking in his direction and he was fairly certain the guy was interested. He was wrong. When he first said hello, the man didn't respond, acting as if he didn't hear him. Rex was fairly sure he did, but said hello again anyway. The man's eyes were ice, and he appeared annoyed. He responded with a cursory "hello" and then continued to stare away. Rex wanted to leave but thought "I can't do that. I'll look like a sad puppy with my tail between my legs." So he stood his ground, but felt increasingly uncomfortable. His mind raced with painful thoughts, one of which was, "Oh my God, I feel like I could just die."

Rejection is certainly uncomfortable but there are degrees of discomfort. There is no argument that Rex was in an awkward position. Yet what was so *terrible* about the situation? He approached someone with the hope of a connection that didn't happen—something that would have absolutely no tangible effect on his life; something that would likely feel half as bad ten minutes later, and not bad at all an hour later—*temporary emotional discomfort that in the scheme of things means absolutely nothing.*

Sometimes just looking at and framing a situation logically can remove most of the sting. Rex could have thought, "OK, I was wrong. He's not interested and this is awkward, but that's it. Nothing catastrophic, nothing horrible. I feel bad, but it won't last long."

As far as not walking away after the so-called rejection, it would have been better if Rex could have thought, "Somehow it seems that

I'm admitting defeat to him by walking away, but that makes no sense. I have no ability to know what he thinks and why should I care about what he thinks anyway? This I do know: I am uncomfortable standing here, and the quicker I leave the quicker I'll feel better. Go now!"

Discomfort Does Not Equal Death

Obviously, most of us don't believe that socially awkward situations will kill us. Yet we use the word "die" often and, as described earlier, powerfully toxic words will have palpably damaging effects. At the very least, phrases such as "this is killing me," and "I can just die right now, I'm so ashamed" create disproportionate, unnecessary psychological anguish. You know that you're not dying but your emotional system doesn't.

Again, Rex could have thought, "I'm real uncomfortable now, but it's tolerable and won't last forever. I'll get through it."

If you are feeling bad after a rejection, listen carefully to what you're telling yourself. If you find any words that describe death, get rid of them.

Approaching As the Goal

One suggestion I give to my therapy clients who struggle with rejection fear is to make the act of *approaching* men, not getting a phone number or otherwise making a connection, the goal.

Although you certainly want to find chemistry with the man you're approaching, whether you do in any specific situation is far less important than the act of approaching. Approaching puts you in contact with others, which provides you with the opportunities that can lead, eventually, to finding a life partner. Yes, if you're hot to trot for someone and he doesn't respond you're going to be upset. But it's important to look at the bigger picture. Not getting laid when you want to is disappointing. Not trying to meet others and remaining unhappily single for years is a lot more troubling.

Making approaching the goal can considerably reduce anxiety. If you tell yourself that you don't have to click with a particular guy, the fear of rejection is less potent because, in a sense, it doesn't matter if you get rejected. Once you initiate contact, you've done what you needed to do. Anything more is gravy.

This doesn't mean that you don't *want* to click. It just means you're controlling the intensity of that desire and acknowledging the value in the act of making the attempt.

It's also very important to give yourself credit for approaching others, no matter what the outcome. Approaching a stranger means you're taking responsibility for getting what you want and are willing to deal with some discomfort. This is laudable. Giving yourself credit will help you feel good about yourself. People who feel good about themselves are likely to feel confident and perform well in social situations. Thus, it may increase your ease with approaching others, and you are more apt to be received well by those you approach. This is a win/win situation.

Start Speaking to Strangers

Many of us, particularly those who live in big cities, shun eye contact with strangers. In New York City, where I grew up, a stranger making eye contact, or G-d forbid, smiling at you, meant one of two things: he was insane, or he was going to rob you!

There are, of course, unsavory characters we all need to avoid. But think of the scores of people you pass every day who are good folks but whom you never look at or make any contact with.

Approaching guys whom you're attracted to can be anxiety producing. The very act of initiating that first exchange with an unfamiliar person is a social skill which necessitates development and practice. Generally speaking, developing and fine-tuning a skill requires preparation in settings with little "risk" or "danger." That's one reason why actors rehearse and orators speak to mirrors.

If you never approach strangers under any circumstances, it is going to be that much more difficult to do so when you feel attracted to one.

Most of the world seems to be in such a constant rush nowadays, that strangers in public settings often look unfriendly. Sometimes they *are* unfriendly, and a smile or any other attempt at small talk on your part will be ignored. Often, however, people find a friendly gesture a refreshing change from the harried, crazy world we all share.

I'm not suggesting you engage in involved conversations with strangers. Simply make contact when you feel the situation is appropriate. For example, you could smile at someone you pass, comment to the person in front or behind you in line at the supermarket, or say "Hello, how are you doing today?" to a waiter or store clerk. There are numerous other opportunities to do this and little downside to the behavior. Although this may not help you practice the more complex conversation you would have with a potential date, it can help you learn how to make initial contact with someone you don't know. This is the first step toward meeting someone and thus very important.

Consider Staying Home When You're Feeling Bad

If you're in a bad mood, it may not be the time to go out. When you're feeling low, you may believe that being around others can help you feel better. That's possible. But if you attempt to meet others and get rejected, it may sour your mood further. Being in a poor mood may also increase you chances of rejection because your mood may be communicated to others. Your mood may serve as a "red flag" warning others to stay away.

If you drink and/or use other drugs, you may get caught up in a cycle that can be very destructive. The cycle goes something like this: bad mood→rejection→worse mood→chemicals (including alcohol) to "medicate" bad feelings→even worse mood→more rejection→even worse mood→more chemicals, and so on.

There Is No Test

One of the worst things you can do is decide that your evening out is going to have a scorecard to face once the night is over. Getting attention and/or phone numbers gives you a high score. No phone numbers, little or no interest means the evening/party/whatever was "a complete failure." What a set up for self-inflicted misery! The fact of the matter is that no social event, no twenty-five social events, are the be all or end all of your life. Approach an event as a time to have fun and *perhaps* meet someone. If you have to do any scoring, showing up and approaching others should give you a *perfect score* because that is the kind of behavior that provides you the greatest chance of reaching your goal of finding a life partner. I am telling you categorically that you're a winner by doing this, not because I'm a therapist and can say only nice things to people (which damn well isn't true!), but because that is the *reality* of the matter. As mentioned previously, a particular guy wanting you or not wanting you is small change in relation to the bigger picture. Being out there, meeting people, taking social risks by approaching others, and living with the discomfort of not always getting what you want is what will eventually lead you to the man of your dreams.

Throughout this book I have stressed that you can get the man you want if you are willing to do the work required. It's foolhardy to limit your horizons and believe in limitations instead of opportunities.

But the man of your dreams has to emerge *from* your dreams if you want him to be in your life. Dreams are all about perfection—humanity is not. Humans are chock-full of faults and weaknesses and limitations.

So how do you find the balance? How do you know you're getting all you can get within the confines of reality? This is not an easy question to answer, particularly for a community that often promotes themes of physical, emotional, and sexual perfection.

But the question begs a response. You may be struggling with this right now as you decide whether to continue with someone you've started to date. You don't want to let the right man slip out of your life. On the other hand, you don't want to forfeit potential opportunities by settling. Let's tackle this in Chapter 11.

Chapter 11

Mr. Perfect Is Not

Kendrick, a financial advisor living in Portland, Oregon, had never sustained a long-term relationship until his forties. Kendrick was exceedingly attractive. At six feet tall, broad and muscular, with large green eyes and sandy brown hair, he had the attention of many men. Kendrick spent a good deal of time working out in the gym and often met men in cruise bars.

A few months after Kendrick's thirty-ninth birthday, his mom, with whom he had been very close, died suddenly of a massive heart attack. Kendrick was in shock, and for the next year took himself out of circulation as he grieved his loss. His "time away" gave him time to look at his life, and he didn't like what he saw. The fast sex, the adoration and attention he received, the "relationships" that went nowhere after the sex went south, were not what he wanted his life to be about. What he did want, however, remained a mystery to him.

After his mother's death, he went out much less and dated only rarely. One day as he was waiting alone in line to see the movie *The Nutty Professor,* a man standing behind him began to talk with him about Eddie Murphy. The man, whose name was Oscar, appeared considerably older than Kendrick. He had gray hair, a gray beard, and many lines on his weather-beaten face. They talked briefly and then parted as they entered the theater. When the movie was over, Kendrick ran into Oscar again as they were exiting. They talked about the movie, and Kendrick found himself laughing as Oscar imitated some of Eddie Murphy's lines. Oscar asked him to coffee. Kendrick told himself that there was no way in hell he would "do anything" with Oscar because he didn't find him physically attractive, but he figured there was little risk in having coffee with the older gentleman. Their impromptu coffee date lasted for about two hours, and Kendrick learned that Oscar was considerably older than him, fifty-five going on fifty-six in another month. Oscar was an elementary school teacher. He had ended a three-year relationship ten months previously. He had had a number of long-term relationships since he was in college, one lasting eight years.

Oscar seemed witty and refreshing, and when he asked for Kendrick's phone number, he did not hesitate to give it to him. In the ensuing six months, they dated, and Kendrick found Oscar different and exciting. To his utter surprise, sex was great. They shared a lot of common interests and values, and Kendrick felt that he was falling in love.

Yet Kendrick had nagging concerns. Oscar didn't look like anyone he'd ever imagined as his lover. Kendrick was a gym bunny, and the man in his dreams was a young, muscular stud in his twenties. Kendrick wondered if years from then he'd be wheeling Oscar around, or bringing him pureed chicken in a nursing home!

Kendrick also made considerably more money than Oscar, and his fantasy of a life partner was an executive in a BMW. Oscar drove a beat-up 1992 Toyota Corolla.

It also didn't help that some of Kendrick's friends referred to Oscar as "gramps."

A crisis ensued on their one-year anniversary. They went to a fancy restaurant to celebrate, and Oscar surprised Kendrick with a ring. Kendrick almost had a panic attack. His eyes opened wide and he turned ashen. Oscar asked him what was wrong. With his mouth quivering, Kendrick said, "I cannot accept this" and literally ran out of the restaurant.

For the next week he refused all attempts by Oscar to contact him. He went through an internal mental hell of trying to figure out what to do. He felt that the ring symbolized a commitment that he was unsure he wanted to make. Oscar was wonderful, but he wasn't what he always imagined his partner would be. He questioned if he was selling himself short. Maybe there's a rich, young, hot guy out there that he'd never meet, he thought. Yet all the signals in his body told him that he wanted to be with Oscar. He wondered if those signals were lying to him. He simply didn't know what to do.

After two weeks, he broke the stalemate and called Oscar. They met on a Sunday afternoon and spent six hours talking. Oscar apologized for putting Kendrick into a bind and Kendrick told him that he had nothing to apologize about. He was honest about his ambivalence and Oscar was open to hearing about it. Oscar told Kendrick that he did not want to force him into a commitment he wasn't ready for. They decided to take one day at a time and see what would happen.

Four years later they are together and both are very happy. Kendrick credits Oscar's ability to hear him out and not make demands as what kept him from running. And Kendrick is happy he didn't. He realized that what really mattered to him was Oscar, not what he now calls a "fantasy of make-believe perfection" in a partner. He has thought throughout the years how much he would have missed if Oscar was not in his life. He chuckles with subtle nervousness when he says that he almost blew the best thing he ever had.

Perfection

Most of us do not actually believe that life can be perfect. Nevertheless, the pursuit of excellence defines American culture. This is as old as the frontier days, and it has served us well. Not being satisfied and reaching for the stars motivates us to better our lives. However, this does not always fare well for relationships.

Physical Perfection

As I discussed earlier, the gay community places enormous value on youth and physical beauty. Much of this is irrational because these attributes have little worth in actually creating and sustaining a relationship. Furthermore, these images are essentially fantasy. Even the hottest of men fart, have bad breath, gain weight, acquire hemorrhoids, break out in rashes, grow old, and die. Hot men occasionally are impotent, tired, frightened, unkempt, not into sex, and a bad lay.

Nevertheless these images remain with us and do harm. Guys who could be right for each other, for example, may never develop anything because each is waiting for the embodiment of youth and physical beauty.

If one should meet and fall in love with a man whose appearance doesn't meet flawlessness standards, the lure of such a vision may create conflict, as it did for Kendrick.

Luckily he didn't run, and instead stayed long enough to figure out what he really wanted.

Falling in love with young, very physically attractive gay men or other kinds of men who depict "male perfection" is certainly possible and magnificent when it happens. Such men, like anyone else, are capable of being good life partners. You may well be such a man. It's the quest for perfection that causes problems. Physical *perfection* images are incompatible with real life, and if your standard is flawlessness no man will satisfy you. Some promising relationships precipitously end when these facts become evident. Often such men "find" irresolvable problems—but what they're really discovering is that the person they're dating is human.

He Will Make You Happy

A relationship that is working will change your life for the better. Love is grounding and ego gratifying, among numerous other positive attributes.

But a partner *will not create* happiness within you. Happiness is the result of an internal activity, a process that enables you to derive joy from the good in life and to cope with the bad. Some of us are better at this than others. Some have significant difficulty because of depression and other problems, and need professional assistance. But the manner by which happiness enters your existence remains forever internal.

Many of us have this backward. We believe the externals of life, such as money, power, and success, will make us happy. It never works that way. Looking at love in this manner will give you the false impression that your partner can "take you away" from your miseries. He won't and he can't. To expect that he will may significantly augment your unhappiness.

Being in love with the right man will enhance the level of contentment in your life. But *enhancing* and *creating* are terribly different phenomena. Clearly appreciating this difference will help you choose reality over fantasy. You don't need a partner to make you happy; nor will you want to leave a partner when he unable to do so.

Meeting All of Your Needs

In a related vein, we sometimes believe that a relationship means having procured a source to meet *all* of our needs. If you had a great mom, she may have tried to do this. Some mothers are truly selfless, and will do for their children everything humanly possible. But the operative word is *human*. Mothers can't protect their children from life. Existence has infinite challenges, and at the end of the day *you, especially you as an adult,* have to navigate the waters to get what you need.

A partner can and should provide a large source of gratification; but he can't anticipate and meet every need you require. You can't always expect him to know when you're sad or frightened, nor to be able to support you, *at all times,* in ways that will help you feel better.

As a relationship develops, each partner may understand how the other is feeling without verbal communication. That's nice when it happens. But lovers are not mind readers, and believing or assuming that such ability is the hallmark of true love is a surefire prescription for serious problems.

Part of why you fall in love is your partner's willingness and ability to be there for you when you really need him. *That should be a given in any viable relationship.* But demanding that he continuously be willing and able to say the right things exactly when you need them to be said is unrealistic.

There are also needs you have that lover will never be able to meet. Perhaps you love opera, or engage in complex political debates, or love to spend hours shopping. You partner may not want nor be able to be involved with any of this. This doesn't mean that you should deny those needs, or that such a relationship can't work. The question you have to ask yourself is this: can those needs be met in other venues, and is that acceptable? Thus, your buddies may provide great opportunities for political debate and your boyfriend can "be left home" when you so want to engage. On the other hand, you may crave a lover who is interested in politics, and to have anything less would not work for you. You have to decide which needs are OK for him *not* to satisfy. That may be difficult to figure out. Take your time and don't sell yourself short. However, if you walk into a relationship believing everything important to you will be satisfied by one individual, you're in for a rude awakening.

You and His "Ugly" Side

Most of us are on our best behavior when we first meet and fall in love. But as our relationship develops, we get to know each other better. One of the most wonderful and scary facts of intimacy is that our social masks eventually fall by the wayside. We get to know with whom we're really involved. If you've done your homework, there's not likely to be much of a shock. Nevertheless, human beings are by nature flawed, and you are guaranteed to witness some ugly stuff.

All of us have dark sides and there is no getting around this fact. We can be petty, vicious, bigoted, insensitive, hateful, vengeful, egocentric, nasty, and disrespectful at times. Sometimes you discover your boyfriend misrepresented who he is. Sometimes the ugly side(s) is more than what you want to deal with. This is when your judgment comes in, and you have to decide whether the relationship is workable. But if you spend enough time with someone, you will find that darker side. It's to be expected.

Likewise, it means you don't have to be the perfect lover. You can relax and let him know who you really are. If he doesn't want you, it means he doesn't want *the real you.* That's a good thing to find out, and the earlier the better. One of the reasons we grow in healthy relationships is because of the supreme validation we get for who we *are.* If your partner is in love with someone he wants you to be, he's not in love with you.

Mistakes

During any day in your life you are likely to make many mistakes. This, of course, is no less true in relationships. We misjudge, don't think, or forget an important date. We occasionally say and do the wrong thing because we're angry at that moment and don't care the hurt we cause. This is true for you and/or your partner. Either one of you is extremely capable of screwing up.

You, of course, have to be the one to decide what is a mistake on your partners part, and to what degree and how many mistakes are acceptable to you. Frequent lying, insensitivity, disrespect, etc., may not be OK, and may more likely be deliberate actions than mistakes.

It's not a sign of maturity or psychological well-being to accept the unacceptable, nor to stay in a relationship that is injurious (Kaminsky, 1999). On the other hand, mistakes will always happen. They can cause considerable pain, and a workable, real relationship means living through the times when you are less than happy and loving toward your partner. It also means accepting your own fallibility and expecting your partner to accept it as well. A relationship devoid of mistakes, including serious ones, is unachievable.

To successfully cope with mistakes, you must recognize that they will happen, and that they are not aberrations indicative of intrinsic flaws, but rather learning experiences both you and your partner can benefit from. Knowing this on an intellectual level in one thing. Not freaking out the first time one of you screws up is another. Thus, it's important to truly prepare yourself for this. Mistakes don't just happen in relationships. Mistakes *will* happen in *your* relationship. *You will be disappointed and hurt at times. You'll displease him now and then.* Expecting mistakes, and believing they can be resolved and even strengthen a relationship, is key to preparing you for a serious relationship.

Harmony and the Lack Thereof

Being in love is about being in sync. It's about having common values and areas of interest. It's about getting along and playing more than working. You shouldn't be involved in something that creates more conflict than connection or is more depleting than replenishing.

Yet being with a life partner is not about perfect consensus either. Two human beings have two perspectives and to think of them as one conscience is frankly scary. You will not always see things the same way. You will disagree and argue.

Two of the weirdest statements I hear from couples is that "We never go to bed angry" and "We seldom argue."

To *never* go to bed angry in any long-term relationship is near impossible. Such an expectation creates enormous pressure that can do much more damage than being pissed and rolling over to the other side of the bed. Indeed, other than a temporary, uncomfortable night, I can't fathom what long-term damage "going to bed angry" will cause.

Men who "never" or "seldom" argue are also worrisome. As a therapist this indicates to me that they are not dealing with conflict. There are many possible reasons for this, *none of which* could be because they never differ. One likelihood is that they have bought into the myth that a successful relationship means perfect harmony. Another possibility is that one or both men may equate disagreements with upheaval and even violence. If this was the experience in one's family of origin, conflict may be feared, and everything is done to avert it.

This doesn't work. Respectfully disagreeing and attempting to problem solve does work.

Couples who never quarrel may harbor growing resentment that comes out, one fine day, in a devastating explosion. Or the small problems that never get aired may grow large, similar to a cancer, and eat away at the foundation of the relationship.

Conflict-free love isn't something you should expect, strive for, or be happy to acquire.

Bumpy and Questioning Times

Any relationship of significant duration will go through good and bad times. The good times should dominate. Perpetual unhappiness is not a "bad phase." But life consistently changes. You get sick, you lose your job, you go through a midlife crisis and question everything.

The healthiest, most "planned out" relationships cannot avoid these changes. The best way to deal with them, besides good communication, is to not be shocked when they visit your relationship.

Frequently, "bumpy times" resolve themselves. When partners don't view this as the beginning of the end, they are more likely to work together and resolve the problem. Sometimes this involves pulling back and letting the other have the space and time to go through whatever it is. When this happens, the relationship changes for the better. The men grow closer, feel stronger in their love, and are better prepared for the next challenge.

Of course, it doesn't always turn out that way.

Being unambiguous about your wants and needs can avert material mistakes in selecting a life partner in the first place. This has been one of the primary themes of this book. But even that cannot prevent the unforeseen.

Sometimes people change in such ways that a once-viable relationship no longer makes sense. No big lapses of judgment, no bad guys, no drama—the relationship simply stops working.

People in unworkable relationships, no matter how much they still love each other, should no longer be there.

I'm not trying to depress you or to tell you that this will happen to your relationship. I'm just saying that it *can,* and that this is a fact of life when you fall in love. Love is not about perfection. It's about life, which is filled with the unforeseen and the unpredictable. Recognizing that this fallibility exists will not only help you live through it if it does, but it can ameliorate the kind of self-attack you may experience. "I've done everything right and still it didn't work—what the hell is wrong with me?" Nothing is wrong with you. It simply happened because these kinds of things happen in relationships.

Falling in love is, in a sense, a dangerous endeavor. When you love, you devote your heart and soul and spirit. They can all be shattered.

Life can get in the way. He can die. He can turn out to be not who he represented himself to be. You can trust and then discover that you've been played the fool.

Trust is an exceedingly complex matter for countless gay men. Many fear trusting, and build walls of "safety." Some take a chance, get wounded, and vow never to let their guard down again. Others behave dishonestly and justify their behavior on grounds that they've been chronically deceived.

There's much pain out there, and reason to be cautious. But there's a fundamental dilemma. Trust is the heart of intimacy: no trust, no intimacy, no relationship.

How you can trust and live with emotional vulnerability is the subject of Chapter 12.

Chapter 12

Embracing Emotional Vulnerability

I met him on the Internet and he seemed very nice. He said and did the right thing and of course I fell for him. Well, he ended up to be a super jerk. A total asshole! Since he was older, he knew how to play me and the game.

Hugh, thirty-two
Social Worker, Kansas City, Missouri

I have friends whom I have gone out with to the bars and (they) have cheated on their boyfriends and lied about it.

Aaron, forty-three
Musician, Cleveland, Ohio

If someone says he's into monogamy, for example, but likes to fuck around, he's really not being terribly honest/available to himself—how could he be for me?

Maxwell, twenty-nine
Waiter, New York, New York

Emotional vulnerability involves openness and defenselessness and exposure of your feelings. Not a joyful thought to consider, since it means that you can be hurt very badly. However, love requires this: *real love* is about deep bonding, and about ungovernable concern, dedication, and care toward another human being. To love and not be emotionally vulnerable is similar to jumping into the ocean and remaining dry. It's unattainable.

No one in his right mind subjects himself to this vulnerability unless he has deep trust—trust not only of one's partner, but trust of the process. Trust that says ultimately you'll be OK no matter what happens.

The words "trust" and "gay men," unfortunately, do not appear often in the same sentence. I have been a gay therapist working with gay men in private practice for over twenty years. Since the publication of my first book, *When It's Time to Leave Your Lover: A Guide for Gay Men,* I have given talks and workshops to many gay men around the country. I have found nothing more constant than the difficulty gay men have with trusting one another.

The stories of "been done wrong to" abound. The pain is tangible, real, and grievous. Yet the men I meet still want a lover. They want it to work out. How can this royal dilemma be resolved?

Internalized Homophobia

The way we feel about being gay, and what we project onto or assume about other gay men, plays a material role in this problem.

One of the principal edicts of homophobia is that gay men are shallow, immature, Peter Pan pseudoadults who cannot be relied upon. "Real men" are the John Wayne/Clint Eastwood types who are always in charge and who never shirk responsibility. Gay men are scared nellies who run at the first sign of danger, who will ditch honesty and boyfriends at the first chance to find someone or something "better."

Most of us regard these ideas as nonsense. We appreciate that they are derivatives of homophobic philosophy and we don't conduct our lives based on them. We also know that some gay men are truly irresponsible and hurtful toward other gay men. That doesn't sound like internalized homophobia. It sounds like reality.

So what am I talking about?

Even though our conscious minds reject homophobic notions, that doesn't mean that the years of exposure to them have no impact. Homophobia remains a potent force in our culture, just as it was when we were growing up. Our logical minds can reject homophobia as our perceptions remain colored by it.

Incidents of being lied to and let down by other gay men are real and probably happened to you. But how you "process" these experiences, how you perceived "gay men" before these incidents happened, and the conclusions you drew from them are vitally significant to your sense of trust—much more so than the incidents themselves.

Growing up in this culture, you were likely to have assumed that gay men would do you wrong long before you knew you were gay, or openly interacted with other gay men. This assumption may still be operating without you even knowing it's there. When you *do* experience true unworthiness, it reinforces this assumption, as opposed to feeling bad *only* toward the specific person who hurt you. Without realizing it, such an experience becomes "evidence" to you that "all gay men" are alike. As you experience more problems or hear horror stories from others, the evidence mounts. You develop and solidify a strong bias not to trust, to consider these men guilty until proven innocent.

Sometimes your perceptions can contradict reality. For example, your boyfriend is in a bad mood and goes to the movies by himself to feel better. But he stays moody. When you ask where he has been, he doesn't feel like telling you, and says "I was out. What's it to you?"

You conclude that he's hiding something, such as fooling around with another guy. You never address it further, and conclude that he's dishonest.

Even more damaging is altering your behavior to accommodate these beliefs. For example, if you conclude that this is "what gay men are like" (all gay men are dishonest), you may decide you should be the same. So you start lying or don't call back when you promise to, or have a clandestine affair while telling your boyfriend he's the only one. The gay men impacted by your poor behavior also see it as evidence of *their* generalized negative feelings about gay men.

So the merry-go-round ensues, and a never-ending, hurtful cycle is cultivated and reinforced.

Getting off that merry-go-round begins by appreciating the role of internalized homophobia. It means literally fighting the tendency to expect dishonesty, and refusing to generalize bad experiences (*no matter how bad and how many of them you had*) to gay men as a whole. It especially means behaving in a manner consistent with trustworthiness and respect.

None of this is easy, and it may require revamping many of your deeply held beliefs. I have found that groups of gay men openly discussing these issues in a safe, supportive atmosphere is one of the best ways to address and transcend these problems. I have seen this take place in the groups I have facilitated.

Reflect on Your Behavior

Many gay men complain about the crap they have handled but say little about what they deal out. As I said in the beginning of this book, unless there's a "secret society of them" it's you and me who are doing what we don't want done to us. It's you and me who can make the change.

I don't suggest engaging in an orgy of self-castigation. This is not about guilt and paying for your crimes. It's about taking a frank look at yourself—what you're doing, what you want, and how you can get it. Are there people you promise to call who you don't? Do you lie? Do you cheat? Do you represent yourself to be someone you're not? If you do engage in this, what are you trying to accomplish? How successful have you been? How do you feel when you "get away with it"? When you don't "get away with it"? Do you believe this is the way everyone behaves? Do you believe this is the only way to get your needs met? Are you afraid to be "played the fool" by being honest?

It is a law of the universe that you get back, generally speaking, what you put out. Sometimes you can get away with things, and life is certainly not fair. But if you engage in dishonest behavior and believe you can attract honest people into your life, you're deluding yourself. We tend to attract those who represent our beliefs. People with low self-esteem, for example, often draw people who aren't affirming. Their outside world becomes a reflection of their internal experience. Likewise, if you see the world in shades of lies and deceit, those are the people you'll find. If you happen to come across someone who is honest, you're likely to perceive him as dishonest nonetheless. Either way, you lose.

Trusting the Process

Being in love is a *guarantee* that you will *not* have control over many powerful emotions.

In a control-driven society, and especially as men, these words are not welcome. Lack of control is very frightening, and because we manage so much in our environment, we often live under the delusion that we can control everything. When it comes to feelings, particularly the mighty perplexing ones associated with love, we're at a loss.

When love works, it is one of the most gratifying experiences a human being can know. Poets, writers, and others have tried for centuries to describe the beauty and intensity of such sentiment.

Of course, when it doesn't work we can be left with loss, anger, confusion, broken dreams, and heartaches about what could have been.

The bad news is that this hurts like hell. The even worse news is that many gay men (and others) do *whatever it takes* to prevent the potential for hurt. Unfortunately "whatever it takes" will take too much. It will *take away your ability to fall in love.* Unless you can trust the process, unless you can live with the uncertainly and the possibility of getting hurt very badly, you will not be able to fall in love.

> The amount that a person is willing to be vulnerable is the amount of intimacy that a person can achieve in the relationship. . . . It (love) does require . . . willingness to be open to being hurt because without that you can't have the good stuff . . .
>
> Brian Wolfe, MFT
> Private Practice, San Francisco, California

The good news is that we don't always need to be in control. We can let go with the knowledge that pain can be manageable, that we don't disintegrate from sorrow, and that anguish can work as wonderful learning experiences. To accept this is liberating.

Obviously you're not going to go from control freak to free spirit over night, and a dialogue about this should begin. Once again, a supportive gay men's group is an excellent way to work through these issues.

Some other good news. It doesn't to take an act of Congress to find or create such a group. If you have a gay community center in your area, ask if a group such as this exists. If not, suggest to the people running the center that you want one. You can also start your own. You may even be able to use space in the gay community center and some of their resources for advertising. Find out. Be creative. Above all, *get off your ass and do something about this.*

Assessing Trustworthiness

> For me the biggest thing is doing what you say you're going to
> do and . . . being able to communicate when you can't. It's about
> agreements. (It's about) being able to keep them or if you need
> to break them . . . to be able to communicate that to the person
> and not just pull the tablecloth out from under them . . .

Brian Wolfe, MFT
Private Practice, San Francisco, California

Adam, a twenty-nine-year-old Chinese-American lab technician met Norman, a thirty-six-year-old Caucasian accountant, at a "new members dinner" of a gay interracial organization in Portland, Oregon. They talked for a long time and exchanged phone numbers. Norman called the following day and left a message. After two days when he hadn't received a call back, he called again and left another message. Ten days later there was still no call back from Adam.

Two months later, Norman ran into Adam in a café. Adam apologized profusely for not calling him back. He said he had been very busy and ended up losing Norman's number. Norman was a little suspicious of the excuse, but decided to ignore his suspicions when Adam asked him for a "second chance." Once again they exchanged phone numbers. This time Adam did call and they went to dinner the following evening. After dinner they went to Norman's house and had sex. Adam said he wanted to see Norman again and thought he was "falling in love." This seemed way too fast and strange to Norman, but he ignored his feelings. He was hot for Adam and thought "what the hell, you live only once—go for it." He was particularly thrilled about the fact that Adam was single. He made it a point to question him about this and Adam was direct and clear. "I am very single and very available, baby."

Norman had been searching for a partner. His boyfriend Thom moved to New York a year ago and he had felt very empty. Adam was cute and smart and Norman thought he'd be a jerk not to pursue him.

Norman called Adam the next day and left a message about what a great time he had had. He asked him if he wanted to get together on the weekend. The weekend came and went with no call back from Adam. On Tuesday evening, he called Adam again and reached him. Adam apologized for not getting back but said he had to work over the weekend. He asked Norman for "another chance" (once again) and Norman readily accepted Adam's invitation to meet for dinner at a local restaurant the following evening at 8 p.m.

Norman finally left at 9 p.m. when Adam had not yet arrived nor called him (on his cell phone). Angry and sad, Norman finally "got it" that Adam was not someone he was going to have a relationship with.

A month later, Norman was having dinner with his friend Trent, when he told him the story of what had happened with Adam. In midsentence Trent dropped his fork, stopped chewing, and stared at Norman with an expression of astonishment and amusement.

"What?" Norman cried.

With a full mouth Trent asked: "This Adam, is he a lab technician?"

"Yes."

"He's about five feet four with a very round, sweet-looking face?"

"Yes."

"He lives downtown?"

"That's him, Trent."

"He's the boyfriend of my co-worker, Lewis! They've been together for three years. Lewis is constantly having trouble with him. That Adam is a lying whore. He's trouble. Stay away from him."

"Thanks for telling me now."

Norman didn't need Trent to tell him about Adam. Adam told him all he needed to know right at the beginning. He then told him again and again. Finally, he told him with a figurative kick in the ass.

Although you have to accept the reality that you can trust and be hurt badly, it doesn't mean that you should unconditionally trust everyone you meet. It's not beneficial to be paranoid, but just as imprudent to be unequivocally blind. In the business of finding a life partner you'll be investing a lot of your soul. You shouldn't waste it on those who don't deserve it.

Developing trust is not a mystifying process in which you hope for the best and say a prayer. There are things you can *do* to assess trustworthiness. Certainly you can work hard at this and still be wrong. On the other hand, good assessing will minimize the likelihood of a bad outcome.

How do you assess? By being attentive. By hearing and seeing what's in front of you. By thinking with your head, not your emotions. *By being alert to your prospective boyfriend's communications.*

Being alert means paying attention to signs no matter how horny and/or lonely you are. Although there are sociopaths in our midst who can fool almost anyone, most people give signals broadcast their trustworthiness or the lack thereof.

A guy who doesn't call back is conveying a powerful, unambiguous message: move on to someone else. This is what Norman should have done.

When Norman didn't hear that message, he got other ones: Adam saying that he "thought he was falling in love" was another such message. People who express feelings out of sync with the length of involvement are usually articulating whims rather than truth. Guys who talk about rearranging the furniture after one or two dates are being dishonest. Perhaps they are mostly lying to themselves, but the effect on you will be no less injurious.

People do make mistakes, and a nice guy could even stand you up on your first date. But unless he was in a plane crash or his toilet caught on fire, a no-show on a first date should mean no second. People are on their best behavior in the beginning. If you see problems at that juncture, the prognosis is poor. In the beginning, it's safest to follow a very simple rule: if it walks and talks like a duck, it's probably a duck.

Those of us who have tolerance for the unacceptable are at risk of ignoring red flags. The thinking usually goes something like this: "I'm being too judgmental. I might miss out if I end this right now. Let me give it a little more time before I make a decision."

You shouldn't, because before you realize it you may have given it a great deal of time. You can become emotionally invested, and becoming involved with someone who's dishonest is maddening, not to mention a desecration of the respect, consideration, and caring you deserve.

Many behavioral indications raise concerned questions about one's honesty and trustworthiness. If you come across these, *particularly when you first meet someone,* consider it bad news. Some of those signs include:

- making contradictory statements, even if they don't appear to be about important topics. He tells you he lives alone and then later mentions he lives with a roommate.
- lying with phony claims at being honest. He first tells you that he broke up with his boyfriend a year ago and then says it was really two weeks ago. He's telling you this *now* because he sees a future with you and wants to be "straight with you." I don't think so.
- appearing grandiose and unbelievable. He's from a rich family, he's a medical doctor, a research scientist, he owns his own plane and a small castle in Brazil. Possible, but not likely.

- being vague about his life—where he lives, what kind of work he does, his relationship history, etc.
- alerting you that he's been and/or currently is dishonest with others—he's with you this night because his boyfriend is out of town and won't find out. Don't think he will be any different with you.
- having a history of being dishonest with previous partners. He confides in you that he has cheated on boyfriends in the past.
- telling you he's irresponsible. He describes how he came to work drunk or how he's walked away from other responsibilities, such as paying bills.
- describing himself as ambitious at the cost of being dishonest. He tells you he socializes with people he detests because it's good for his career.
- thinking lying is OK to "protect " others.
- having friends who engage in dishonest behavior and he has no problem with it.
- observing him to behave dramatically differently with different people. He's very caring and sensitive with you but nasty and demanding with a waiter.
- appearing manipulative—he seems to be stroking your ego because he wants you to have sex with him or he wants something else from you.
- expressing intense "feelings" that seem out of proportion with the reality of the situation (as described previously)—you've had two dates and he's talking about moving in because he's "falling in love."
- *asking* you to buy him a drink, dinner, etc. It's very different if you *offer* this.
- not calling back/not showing up/not coming through with what he told you he'd do short of a serious, verifiable reason. His car breaks down and you meet him at the gas station after he calls is reasonable. He forgets to meet you is not.
- having multiple combinations of this list. *People having difficulty following through with what they say they'll do, no matter what excuses they provide, is one of the most ominous indications of dishonesty.* "Showing up" both figuratively and literally,

is enormously important, and if he can't do that he can't "do" a relationship.

Your History with Trust and Honesty

Let's suppose you don't encounter the worrisome signs just described. What if you meet a seemingly decent man? What if he calls back, shows up, tells the truth, is unguarded, doesn't have a secretive life, has respectable friends, and wants to be with you? Should you trust him?

You should. People who evidence honesty, dependability, consistency, and candor among other positive traits are the ones you should give a chance. As I've said repeatedly, there are no guarantees but the business of love is not about guarantees. It's about taking sensible, reasonable chances. Developing trust with guys who possess positive attributes is doing just that.

But what if you *can't* trust him, no matter how much you would like to?

Forging a sense of trust is a crucial developmental task that we hopefully accomplish during our early years. In the ideal situation, your parents or parental figures consistently came through when you needed them. From those experiences you not only see others as trustworthy, but enjoy a broad feeling that the world is a safe place.

Many of us never had the ideal, and for some, everything *but* the ideal. Traumatic experiences such as sexual abuse, physical abuse, neglect, and abandonment can shatter a child's developing sense of trust. Less dramatic but nonetheless serious problems such as an emotionally unavailable parent can cause significant problems with trust.

Trauma can also visit you as an adult. Some relationships turn very ugly, and we may be deeply betrayed by someone we "thought we knew." I knew a couple in Miami who split up after being together for fourteen years. While one was close to death on a ventilator after a serious suicide attempt, the other was busy with his lawyer arranging the dissolution of their mutual property. He didn't call, visit, or inquire about his partner's status as he lay dying.

Trauma both as a child and as an adult can make it very difficult to trust anyone. Since a love relationship is one of the most intense forms of bonding, a person with such a history will be terrified at the prospect of falling in love. Trust to such a person is perceived as exceptionally perilous and downright foolish. This thinking may not be conscious but its effects are palpable nevertheless. Those who don't transcend such traumas are likely to remain embittered and lonely. They tend to stay single and resentful, bond with treacherous characters who further abuse them, or find an honest soul whom they can't trust and eventually push away.

If you find that it's very difficult to trust anyone, and/or you become consistently involved with dishonest people, I suggest you seek professional help. An honest guy is not going to change your feelings, and those feelings will nourish an invisible but impenetrable barrier between yourself and a real life partner. It need not be there.

Perhaps you've come a long way by now. You're taking responsibility for your happiness and are seriously looking for a life partner. You know the places to find men, especially the places you're comfortable with. You've mourned your losses and moved beyond ex-lovers. You figured out what you want and need in a partner, and know how to spot someone who's available for a relationship. You appreciate what a real relationship is about and are not expecting the Hollywood version. You've dealt with rejection and can walk up to any man you want.

It's time for you to be dating!

Dating is a wonderful/scary/exciting/depressing/hopeful/confusing/exhilarating time and much more. It brings you in contact with "wrong numbers" guys that are good just for sex, men you want but who don't want you, and the possibility of meeting a life partner.

How do you negotiate this period in your life in a way that will augment your chances of finding a lover? How do you cope with the frustration of meeting guys who will not become your life partner? Should you date more than one man at a time? How do you express interest without scaring him off? What part should feelings play and what part should "logic" figure into your decisions? How will you know that he's *the one?* Is there an absolute way to know that? *What kind of information will he give you in this early phase that will go a long way in letting you know if he's right for you?*

Let's look at all of this and more in Chapter 13.

Chapter 13

Dating for Your Future

Dating is frequently depicted as a carefree time with lots of fun, easy sex, and no commitments. For some it is. But if you're looking for a partner, you may not welcome this. You want to find your man, and each time he's a no-show you may feel frustrated and even hopeless.

One of the best ways to get through this is to accept that dating is about peaks and valleys. Courting is likely to lead to many blind alleys before it leads you to the right door. You could conceivably find him on the first date but then you'd have another problem—you may wonder if you gave yourself enough choice before you settled. So take a deep breath and go with it. What you *shouldn't* do is conclude after a few or even many "wrong numbers" that he's not out there. He is—you just have to meet those frogs before you find your prince!

Furthermore, *going down blind alleys is part of the process of finding him.* The wrong guys demonstrate in clear, bold relief what you *don't* want. This helps sharpen your judgment. You may think that a guy who's overly focused on success is not for you, but when you actually go out with someone such as this, your resolution becomes strengthened. This aids you in identifying the right man when he does come your way.

Anxiety and Insecurity

Dating is a time of experimentation and exploration with little commitment. You and your dates owe nothing to each other and either of you can bail at any time. If you find yourself excited about someone this can be frightening. What, you may wonder, if he's not equally thrilled? Once again, there's little you can do but go with it.

Either he will discover that he feels the same or he won't. One way you can manage this is to keep in mind that no one man is the only guy who can be your future life partner. If it doesn't work out it will be disappointing, but you simply have to get back up on the horse and try again.

Some guys, particularly those who have been searching for a long time, become obsessed when they find a man they are excited about. They feel they must do everything and anything to make sure he doesn't "slip away." This approach is bound to backfire. This intensity is likely to communicate desperation, which will cause any psychologically healthy man to run for the hills and rapidly ascend them.

Often, in a situation such as this, one may attempt to create a false persona to win the person's heart. You may voice opinions you don't have, express interest in activities you're not interested in, and so on. Although we are all on our best behavior when we first date, trying to be who you aren't is a different animal. Aside from creating self-eseem poison, this can interfere with your appraisal of who *he* is. Your focus on meeting his needs can cause you to ignore your own. You may miss vital information that reveals incompatibility. Indeed, your excitement may be more about your longing to have a lover than having actually found him. What's more, you can be someone else for only so long. If he falls in love with a false sense of who you are, he's in for a bad shock once he gets to know the real you. And that is inevitable. Denying one's real self in the pursuit of another does not work.

Opening Up

Dating is about getting to know someone and letting him discover you. But what's too much or too little disclosure?

Although you should never present a false depiction, this doesn't mean you reveal your life story over your first cup of coffee. Letting it all out immediately is inappropriate because it implies a certain amount of intimacy that has not been developed. This also communicates an expectation of familiarity the other person has not yet agreed to.

On the other hand, as you date someone over a period of time, it's important to go beyond facades so you each get to know the other. Letting almost nothing out will impede the development of intimacy. Being open not only enables the learning to progress, *but it's the very process that will create a relationship* (if the ingredients to bond are there). *People fall in love with other people, not Madison Avenue images.*

So when do you do what? This is the kind of question I often encounter when I speak to groups. Unfortunately, I don't have that magic formula. It is a judgment call, and you have to decide how comfortable you are with revealing the deeper parts of yourself. What constitutes the "deeper parts" is also a personal decision. Generally speaking, they are the more real parts, the ones less determined by social expectations and more connected to the unique person you are.

One measure to look at, however, is time. If you've been seeing someone for a number of weeks and feel you're at the same level as on your first date, take a close look at that. The other issue is your comfort with intimacy or lack thereof. Significant problems with getting close to others must be resolved in order to find a partner.

Do You Let Him Know You Really Like Him?

If after a period of time you find that you're developing strong feelings for someone, do you let him know?

Some fear this will scare a guy away and that it's always best to play "hard to get." I disagree.

If your feelings are genuine and not fleeting infatuation, it's important to reveal it. By "genuine" I mean that significant time has passed, you have good insight, and you *know* your feelings are real. If that's going to make him run, it's best to find out sooner rather than later. Being mature enough for a relationship means not running from the expression of strong feelings. Furthermore, he may feel the same about you. If you both remain silent about the good news, you may never develop the relationship that could have been. What a waste, all because both of you were afraid! Go for it and let the chips fall where they may. If he doesn't feel the same way and sees no future with you, it will hurt but that's also *good* news. What do I mean? You can start the painful but *necessary* process of pulling back and looking for a guy who will love you the way you love him. It's a terrible waste to be in love with someone who's not in love with you. You deserve better.

Single or Multiple Dating?

"Multiple dating" as defined here, means seeing a number of different men at the same time.

There are good arguments for and against. Going out with a few men at a time gives you access to more men. Finding a lover is, *to some degree,* a numbers game. The more men you're exposed to, the more likely you'll encounter the one you're seeking.

Furthermore, seeing different guys gives you different experiences that you can compare. It can help you clearly define what you're seeking and what doesn't work for you.

On the other hand, dating a few guys at a time may be confusing. Feelings may creep in and you could be faced with falling for more than one guy.

It can also be, conversely, a way to prevent you from developing any strong feelings. If you are afraid to get close because of previous bad experiences, for example, this can serve as a way to "protect" you. You keep a psychological arm's length from each guy as you tell yourself that you're simply playing the field. As you begin to sense potential feelings for one guy, you switch your focus to another. This is a grand way of getting nowhere. This dynamic may be operating without your conscious awareness of it. One way to figure this out is to take a frank look at what getting close to a new man means for you. Is it terrifying? Do you fear reliving a previous bad relationship? Are you not over your ex and feel that falling in love would put finality on your breakup? If any of this is happening, you need to address your fear. Multiple dating is probably not a good idea for you. "More" in this case is really less, and no matter how many men you see, a life partner will remain elusive as long as fear remains unresolved.

If you do see more that one guy at a time (assuming the previous description doesn't apply to you), you should let each guy know what's going on. The most important reason for this is that it means you're being honest. Yes, some guys may not want to date you if you're dating others. But to date them when they have a false understanding means starting out with dishonesty. Nothing good can come from that. Being honest creates one of the healthiest foundations for a relationship. You may "lose" some dates, but in the long run you'll attract the right guys.

If you want to date only one man at a time but he wants to see others, you have to decide whether to continue with him. Dating others when you don't want to makes no sense (just because he's doing it), and you can't expect him not to see others if that's what he wants.

Once again, honesty is imperative. Being honest on both sides means each of you knows what's going on, and each has the best chance of making an appropriate decision.

A Time of Evaluation

The period of dating is an important time to make decisions. It's during this phase when you will choose whether the man you're seeing will be your partner. Of course that's only half of the equation. He will have to come to the same conclusion. Although it is important to be discussing this with him as the days turn to weeks and months, in a sense this has to be two unilateral decisions. You have to decide for *yourself* if he's the one, and he needs to do the same. Should you feel he is and he feels likewise, you have a relationship. If not, you don't. But without knowing the final outcome, you still have to do some serious soul-searching. You have your work cut out for you.

Thoughts and Feelings

Your decision will be based on feelings and on thoughts. Both are important. The best guy on "paper" is meaningless if you don't *feel* that special chemistry that makes you excited and in love. But your thinking—does this guy meet your needs, is he emotionally available, will he be there when the music stops—is equally essential. Furthermore, thinking will affect feelings. A guy who demonstrates irresponsibility may assuage the development of strong affection. Likewise, someone who exhibits other good qualities may augment a burgeoning passion.

When to Begin Assessing

As dating progresses to a more serious stage, that is, considerable time has passed, neither one of you is seeing others, and you're both talking about a future, you need to resolve important questions. The time to begin addressing these questions, however, was before you reached this stage. Day one of a relationship is when you should start. You will, of course, have less information in the beginning. But watching very early on sets the tone and stage for getting into serious relationships with your head screwed on right. Countless relationships land in the trash bin of regrets and broken dreams because no one wanted to *think* as they rode on the highs of passion. Those feelings are wonderful, and I'm not saying you shouldn't bask in the glory of their visit; however, the scale must be balanced with doses of reality. Clear thinking is essential if you want a *real* life partner.

Naturally, as you get more serious you will be able to explore these questions in more depth. This process should give you the answers you need to make your decision.

Many factors that turn out to be relationship clinchers or relationship sinkers are obvious in the very beginning. You just have to keep your eyes open. Furthermore, you have to have the resolve to walk away from something that feels good but which you know is futile. *When you spend time and energy on someone who's not right, you rob yourself of the opportunity to find someone who is.*

The Questions

Much of what we addressed in the previous pages must now be applied to this possible life partner. To begin with, *are you ready, willing, and able to make a commitment to another human being? Is this the right time in your life to get involved?* Impatience is a very American trait, but it's not the way to start a healthy relationship. If you're not ready, you're not ready. Give yourself the time and whatever else you need to be in the right mind-set for a lover.

If you are ready, what are you needs and wants and is he/will he be able to meet them? Is he psychologically available? Is he emotionally mature? Does he share your values and outlook? What's different and similar and how will that fare? Are you sexually satisfied? Can you communicate? Is time with him more fun than work? Is he a friend in addition to a lover?

These are but a few of the many questions that need to be addressed before you can commit to commit. Before we conclude, here are a few more that are essential. This list is not exhaustive; only you know what's vitally important to you, so feel free to add your own.

* What is his relationship history? Has he been seriously involved with someone and for how long?
* How did he uncouple? Why? How long ago? Is he over his ex?
* Is he at the same level of intelligence as you?
* How do you communicate?

- Do you feel understood?
- Do you feel supported?
- How does he behave when he's angry, tired, frustrated?
- What part does his career play in his life? How will that affect you? How does it affect you now?
- What are his thoughts about honesty? What is his history with honesty? Does he tell you the truth?
- What do you think of his friends?
- To what level is he out of the closet? How does that fare with your openness or lack thereof?
- What is his relationship with his family? What role do you see yourself having with his family? How do feel about that?
- Is he content with where he is now living, or does he plan to re-locate in the near future? If so, how do you feel about moving?
- Is there a significant age difference? Are you from different eth-nic, religious, class backgrounds? How will any/all of this im-pact your relationship? Have you addressed these issues as a couple?
- How he does he see day-to-day life in a relationship? How does this compare with your view?
- Does he follow through? Does he show up, call back, and re-member what he promises, not just to you but also to others?
- How does he treat waiters and taxi drivers and anyone who may be in a less powerful position than he is in?
- Is he physically healthy? Does he take care of himself, go to the dentist, do drugs, smoke, etc., and how does this matter or not matter to you?

In Conclusion

On the morning of September 11, 2001, I was working on this manuscript at about five in the morning, a common time for me to write. When I finished, about 6:30 a.m. PST, I turned on the television and was shocked at what I saw. One of the World Trade Center towers was engulfed in flames. I thought to myself that it was quite a large fire but surmised that it had started inside the building. I had not real-ized within those first seconds that it was the result of a plane crash.

The rest, of course, is history. I watched in horror as the second plane crashed. I saw two towers crumble to the ground. I was literally screaming at this point into the answering machine of my partner. Although we are both on the West Coast my first impulse was to make certain he was safe. He was at a local gym and called back shortly. My stress level went from a 100 to 0.

That night we had dinner. Although I felt profound sadness about the innocent people who perished, and anger at those who visited this upon us, I also felt like the luckiest man on earth. I was alive, so was my partner, and we were sitting together sharing a meal. "How fortunate we are," I said to him.

Your lover is there to laugh when you stub your toe, share a hot chocolate with on a snowy Christmas, and make love with you in the dead of night. He's there when the world has lost all semblance of sanity and you need an anchor against the darkness. He's there to hear about your crazy day, your terrible job, and your car that caught on fire. He's there to share your triumphs and make the sweetness of your successes even sweeter. He's there to be in your history, your photographs, your memories, and your soul. He's there to care about and love you, as you are there to care about and love him.

This and a whole lot more lie ahead when love is in your life.

And you can find that love. He's really out there and he wants to find you. You just have to decide that you're going to meet him.

Not try to, nor hope to, nor want to.

Decide you're going to find him.

This means making peace with the work, time investment, and blind alleys you'll encounter. It means self-legitimizing your longing for a lover, and being willing to let the world know you want him. It means refusing to let age, looks, and fear impede your quest. It means extricating the poison and dead-end mentality of negative expectations and internalized homophobia. It means believing that your past cannot and *will not* limit your future. It means daring to dream and doing what it takes to make your dreams the soul of your life.

Your life-partner-to-be may be reading this book as you are now. You're both good men who have much to offer. Your lives are complete and happy, but together you'll soar. You have a relationship to form, a future to create, a history to remember and cherish.

So put down this book, take a deep breath, and go out and meet him.

When you do, tell him Neil sent you.

Good luck!

Bibliography

Alexander, Christopher J. *Growth and Intimacy for Gay Men: A Workbook*. Binghamton, NY: The Haworth Press, 1997.

Berger, Raymond M. *Gay and Gray: The Older Homosexual Man*, Second Edition. Binghamton, NY: The Haworth Press, 1996.

Bourne, Edmund J. *The Anxiety and Phobia Workbook*. Oakland, CA: New Harbinger Publications Inc., 1995.

Davis, Martha, McKay, Matthew, and Robbins Eshelman, Elizabeth. *The Relaxation and Stress Reduction Workbook*. Oakland, CA: New Harbinger Publications, 1982.

De Becker, Gavin. *The Gift of Fear: Survival Signals That Protect Us from Violence*. New York: Dell, 1998.

Duberman, Martin. *Stonewall*. New York: The Penguin Group, 1993.

George, Kenneth. *Mr. Right Is Out There: The Gay Man's Guide to Finding and Maintaining Love*. Los Angeles, CA: Alyson Books, 2000.

Hardin, Kimeron N. *The Gay and Lesbian Self-Esteem Book: A Guide to Loving Ourselves*. Oakland, CA: New Harbinger Publications, Inc., 1999.

Isensee, Rik. *Are You Ready? The Gay Men's Guide to Thriving at Midlife*. Los Angeles, CA: Alyson Books, 1999.

Jones, Anderson. *Men Together: Portraits of Love, Commitment and Life*. Philadelphia, PA: Running Press Book Publishers, 1997 (photographs by David Fields).

Kaminsky, Neil. *When It's Time to Leave Your Lover: A Guide for Gay Men*. Binghamton, NY: The Haworth Press, 1999.

Miller, Scott D., Duncan, Barry L., and Hubble, Mark A. *Escape from Babel: Toward a Unifying Language for Psychotherapy Practice*. New York: W.W. Norton and Company, 1997.

Oxford American Dictionary. Carruth, Gorton, Ehrlich, Eugene, Flexner, Stuart Berg, Hawkins, Joyce, M. Eds. New York: Oxford University Press Inc., 1980.

Index

SPECIAL 25%-OFF DISCOUNT!
Order a copy of this book with this form or online at:
http://www.haworthpressinc.com/store/product.asp?sku=4758

AFFIRMATIVE GAY RELATIONSHIPS
Key Steps in Finding a Life Partner

_____in hardbound at $29.96 (regularly $39.95) (ISBN: 1-56023-362-1)

_____in softbound at $14.96 (regularly $19.95) (ISBN: 1-56023-363-X)

Or order online and use Code HEC25 in the shopping cart.

COST OF BOOKS_____

OUTSIDE US/CANADA/
MEXICO: ADD 20%_____

POSTAGE & HANDLING_____
*(US: $5.00 for first book & $2.00
for each additional book)
Outside US: $6.00 for first book
& $2.00 for each additional book)*

SUBTOTAL_____

IN CANADA: ADD 7% GST_____

STATE TAX_____
*(NY, OH & MN residents, please
add appropriate local sales tax)*

FINAL TOTAL_____
*(If paying in Canadian funds,
convert using the current
exchange rate, UNESCO
coupons welcome)*

☐ **BILL ME LATER:** ($5 service charge will be added)
(Bill-me option is good on US/Canada/Mexico orders only;
not good to jobbers, wholesalers, or subscription agencies.)

☐ Check here if billing address is different from
shipping address and attach purchase order and
billing address information.

Signature_____

☐ **PAYMENT ENCLOSED: $**_____

☐ **PLEASE CHARGE TO MY CREDIT CARD.**

☐ Visa ☐ MasterCard ☐ AmEx ☐ Discover
☐ Diner's Club ☐ Eurocard ☐ JCB

Account # _____

Exp. Date_____

Signature_____

Prices in US dollars and subject to change without notice.

NAME_____

INSTITUTION_____

ADDRESS_____

CITY_____

STATE/ZIP_____

COUNTRY_____ COUNTY (NY residents only)_____

TEL_____ FAX_____

E-MAIL_____

May we use your e-mail address for confirmations and other types of information? ☐ Yes ☐ No
We appreciate receiving your e-mail address and fax number. Haworth would like to e-mail or fax special
discount offers to you, as a preferred customer. **We will never share, rent, or exchange your e-mail address
or fax number.** We regard such actions as an invasion of your privacy.

Order From Your Local Bookstore or Directly From
The Haworth Press, Inc.
10 Alice Street, Binghamton, New York 13904-1580 • USA
TELEPHONE: 1-800-HAWORTH (1-800-429-6784) / Outside US/Canada: (607) 722-5857
FAX: 1-800-895-0582 / Outside US/Canada: (607) 722-6362
E-mail to: getinfo@haworthpressinc.com
PLEASE PHOTOCOPY THIS FORM FOR YOUR PERSONAL USE.
http://www.HaworthPress.com   BOF02